D0032920

ROME SWEET HOME

Scott and Kimberly Hahn. July, 1993.

Rome Sweet Home

OUR JOURNEY TO CATHOLICISM

Scott and Kimberly Hahn

IGNATIUS PRESS   SAN FRANCISCO

Cover design by Riz Boncan Marsella

© 1993 Ignatius Press
ISBN 0–89870–478–2
Library of Congress catalogue number 93–79336
Printed in the United States of America

CONTENTS

With gratitude to God for our parents
Jerry and Patricia Kirk
Molly Lou Hahn
and in loving memory of Fred Hahn

Thanks for the gifts of life and love.
It's a privilege to honor you as son and daughter.

With gratitude to God for our children
Michael Scott
Gabriel Kirk
Hannah Lorraine
Jeremiah Thomas Walker

You are God's gifts of life and love,
making us a family.
It's a joy to be your mom and dad.

Foreword

One of the beautiful and bright-shining stars in the firmament of hope for our desperate days is this couple, Scott and Kimberly Hahn, and this story of their life and their conversion. It is one of increasingly many such stories that seem to be springing up today throughout the Church in America like crocuses poking up through the spring snows.

All conversion stories are different—like snowflakes, like fingerprints. But all are dramatic. The only story even more dramatic than conversion to Christ's Church is the initial conversion to Christ himself. But these two dramas—becoming a Christian and becoming a Catholic—are two steps in the same process and in the same direction, like being born and growing up. This book is an excellent illustration of that truth.

Because of the intrinsic drama of its subject—man's quest for his Creator and his for him—*all* conversion stories are worth listening to. But not all arrest you and sweep you along like a powerful river as this one does. I can think of four reasons for the un-put-down-able-ness of this book.

First, the authors are simply very bright, clear-thinking and irrefutably reasonable. I would hate to be an anti-Catholic in debate against these two!

Second, they are passionately in love with Truth and

with honesty. They are incapable of fudging anything except fudge.

Third, they write with clarity and simplicity and charity and grace and wit and enthusiasm and joy.

Fourth, they are winsome and wonderful people who share themselves as well as the treasure they have found. When you meet them in the pages of this book, you will meet that indefinable but clearly identifiable quality of *trustability*. The Hebrews called it *emeth*. When you touch them, you know you touch truth.

There are also religious reasons for this book's power.

One is its evident love of Christ. It's as simple as that.

Another is its love and knowledge of Scripture. I know no Catholics in the world who know and use their Bible better.

A third is their Christlike combination of traditional biblical and Catholic orthodoxy with modern personalism and sensitivity—in other words, love of truth *and* of people, both the subject and the student. This double love is the primary secret of great teachers.

Finally, there is their theological focus on the family, both biological and spiritual (the Church as family). This doctrine, like each item of the Church's wisdom, gets defined and appreciated most clearly when threatened by heresies that deny it. Today this fundamental foundation of all human and divine society is under attack and seems to be dying before our eyes. Here are two warriors in the army of Saint Michael the Archangel as he counterattacks old Screwtape's latest invasion. The tide of battle is turning, and the Church's sea of wisdom is readying itself to flood and wash our land of its defilement. Scott and Kimberly are two early waves of that cleansing tide.

There are no tapes more in demand and more extensively and enthusiastically shared among American Catholics today than the Hahn tapes. Now we have the full version of their story. It will be met with spiritual mouths as open as those of young robins.

PETER KREEFT

Preface

The late Archbishop Fulton Sheen once wrote: "There are not over a hundred people in the United States who hate the Roman Catholic Church; there are millions, however, who hate what they wrongly believe to be the Catholic Church."

Both of us once thought that we belonged in the former group, only to discover that we were really in the latter. But once we saw the distinction, and where we really were, it slowly became apparent that we did not belong in either group. By then we were well on our way home. This book describes that journey. It is a narrative of how we discovered the Catholic Church to be God's covenant family.

Our focus in this book is on how the Holy Spirit used Scripture to clear up *our* misconceptions; we have not attempted to deal with all the misconceptions that others may have. By God's grace maybe someday we can write a book with that in mind.

This story could not have been written except for Terry Barber of Saint Joseph Communications, West Covina, California, who generously provided a notebook computer along with many different tapes of our talks for Kimberly to transcribe and edit into a readable form. Incidentally, she did all of her work upstairs, where three children and a toddler were roaming about, while Scott was tucked away in a quiet corner of the basement working to complete his doctoral dissertation, "Kinship by Covenant". By his own admission, Scott's authorial absenteeism accounts for whatever obtuseness remains.

G. K. Chesterton once said, "If something is *really* worth doing . . . it's worth doing badly!" That explains our reason for—and consolation in—taking the risk to share our journey in print at this very busy time of our lives.

Scott and Kimberly Hahn
Feast of Saints Peter and Paul
June 29, 1993

Introduction

We thank God for the grace of our conversion to Jesus Christ and the Catholic Church which he founded; for it is only by the most amazing grace of God that we could ever have found our way home.

I, Scott, thank God for Kimberly, the second most amazing grace in my life. She is the one whom God used to reveal to me the reality of his covenant family; and while I am enthralled with the theory, Kimberly puts it into practice, joyfully serving as the channel for God's third most amazing graces: Michael, Gabriel, Hannah and Jeremiah. The Lord has used these forenamed graces to help this bumbling biblical detective (the "Columbo of Theology") crack the case of Catholicism—by coming home.

In truth, the journey began as a detective story, but soon it became more like a horror story, until it finally ended up as a great romance story—when Christ unveiled his Bride, the Church. (By the way, it would help to keep these three story types in mind as you read.)

I, Kimberly, thank God for my beloved husband, Scott. He has taken seriously God's call to nourish me with the Word of God and to cherish me by the grace of God (Eph 5:29). He has paved the way for our family to be received into the Church by laying down his life—education, dreams, career—for us, because he followed Christ no matter what the cost.

As with Scott's pilgrimage, mine altered in tone and color as it progressed, like the change of seasons. Little did I know how long it would be from summer to spring.

The Hahn family, 1975. Scott is in top right corner.

From the Cradle to Christ

Scott:

I was the youngest of three Hahn children born to Molly Lou and Fred Hahn. Baptized a Presbyterian, I was raised in a nominal Protestant home. Church and religion played a small role in my life and for my family, and then mostly for social reasons rather than any deep convictions.

I recall the last time I ever attended our family's church. The minister was preaching all about his doubts regarding the Virgin Birth of Jesus and his bodily Resurrection. I just stood up in the middle of his sermon and walked out. I remember thinking, I'm not sure what I believe, but at least I'm honest enough not to stand up and attack the things I'm supposed to teach. I also wondered, Why doesn't the man just leave his ministry in the Presbyterian church and go wherever his beliefs are held? Little did I know that I had witnessed a portent of my own future.

Whatever I did, I did it with passion, whether right or wrong. A typical teenager, I lost all interest in the church and became very interested in the world. Consequently, I soon found myself in deep trouble; labeled a delinquent, I had to appear in juvenile court. Faced with a yearlong sentence to a detention center for a variety of charges, I barely lied my way out of the sentence and into six months of probation instead. Unlike my best friend,

Dave, I was scared of where things were headed. I knew things had to change. My life was headed downhill fast, and I was out of control.

I noticed that Dave was nonchalant. I knew that he was a Catholic, but when he boasted about lying to the priest in confession, I thought I'd heard it all. Talk about hypocrisy! All I could say was, "Dave, I'm sure glad that I'll never have to confess my sins to a priest." Little did I know.

My first year of high school the Lord brought into my life a university student named Jack. He was a leader in Young Life, a parachurch ministry founded to share the gospel with hard-core, unchurched kids, like me and my friends. Jack became a good friend, and our relationship meant a lot to me. He'd shoot hoops and hang out with us after school and then give us rides home in his van.

After getting to know me, Jack invited me to a Young Life meeting. I politely said, "Thanks, but no thanks." I had no intention of going to some religious meeting, even if it wasn't church.

Then Jack mentioned that a certain girl named Kathy was coming. He must have known that Kathy happened to be the girl I was trying to hustle at the time; so I told him, "I'll think about it." Then he went on to say that one of the finest guitarists in Pittsburgh, a fellow named Walt, played at their meetings and stuck around afterward to jam with any interested guitar players. That year, as Jack well knew, guitar had practically become my religion, replacing less worthwhile pursuits. At least, now I could offer my friends a valid excuse for going to Young Life.

So I went. I talked to Kathy awhile, and I jammed with Walt, who was truly amazing on the guitar. He even showed me a few licks. The next week I was back—and the next and the next.

Each week Jack would give a talk in which he made one of the gospel stories about Jesus come to life. Then he'd challenge us with the basic message of the gospel: we were sinners in need of salvation, and Christ died on the Cross to pay for our sins. We had to choose him as our personal Lord and Savior to be saved—it wasn't automatic. I listened, but I wasn't very impressed.

About a month later Jack asked me to go on a retreat. I said, "No, thanks, I've got other plans!" Then he told me that Kathy would be there—for the whole weekend. Smart guy. My "other plans" could wait.

The retreat speaker presented the gospel in a simple but challenging way. On the first night he said, "Take a look at the Cross. And if you are tempted to treat your sins lightly, I want you to take a hard, long look." He made me realize for the first time that, yes, my sins were what put Jesus on the Cross.

The next night he challenged us in another way. He said, "If you are tempted to treat the love of God lightly, look again at the Cross, because it's God's love that sent Christ there for you." Up to that point I had thought of God's love as sentimental. But the Cross is anything but sentimental.

The man then called us to make a commitment to Christ. I saw a number of my peers all around respond, but I held back. I thought, I don't want to get all caught up in the emotion. I'll wait. If this stuff is true tonight, it'll be true in a month. So I went home, postponing any decision to commit my life to Christ.

I had purchased two books on the retreat. One night, a month later, I read *Know Why You Believe*, by Paul Little, all the way through and sections of C. S. Lewis' *Mere Christianity*. These books answered many of my questions about things like evolution, the existence of God, the possibility of miracles, the Resurrection of Jesus and the reliability of Scripture. Around two in the morning, I turned off the light, rolled over and prayed, "Lord Jesus, I am a sinner. I believe you died to save me. I want to give my life to you right now. Amen."

I went to sleep. There were no angel choirs, trumpet blasts or even a rush of emotions. It all seemed so un-eventful—but the next morning, when I saw the two books, I remembered my decision and prayer. I knew something was different.

My friends also noticed something was different. My best friend, Dave, who was one of the most popular kids in school, found out I wasn't willing to do dope any more. He took me aside and said, "Scott, no offense, but we don't want you hanging around with us any more. Me and the guys think you're a narc."

I said, "C'mon, Dave, you know I'm not a narc."

"Well, we don't know what you are, but you've changed and we don't want you around any more. Have a nice life!" And off they went.

I was stunned. About a month after making this com-mitment to Christ, I found myself alone, without a friend in the high school. I felt betrayed. I turned to God and said, "Lord, I gave you my life and you've taken away my friends. What kind of deal is this?"

Though I couldn't have known it at the time, God was calling me to sacrifice something that stood in the way of my relationship to him. It was hard and slow, but over the next two years I developed solid friendships that were real and true.

Before finishing my sophomore year, I experienced the transforming power of God's grace in conversion. Within the next year, I experienced a special outpouring of the Holy Spirit in a personal and life-changing way. As a result, I acquired an insatiable hunger for Scripture. I fell head over heels in love with the Word of God—the inerrant, infallible guide to our life as Christians—and with the study of theology.

I devoted the last two years of high school to playing the guitar and studying Scripture. Jack and his friend Art taught me Scripture. Art even brought me along to some of his seminary classes with Dr. John Gerstner in my senior year.

I decided the figures in Christian history who most appealed to me—and the ones Jack and Art were always talking about—were the great Protestant reformers Martin Luther and John Calvin. I first studied how Martin Luther rediscovered the gospel, or so I thought, completely separating himself from the Catholic Church. I began to devour his works.

As a consequence, I became very strong in my anti-Catholic convictions. I was so firmly convinced that for Miss Dengler's English class in high school I decided to write my senior research paper on Luther's views. As a result, I had a mission to correct and to liberate Catholics bound up with unbiblical works-righteousness legalism. Luther had convinced me that Catholics believed they were saved by their works but that the Bible taught justification by faith alone, or *sola fide*.

Luther once declared from the pulpit that he could commit adultery one hundred times in a day and it would not affect his justification before God. Obviously this was rhetorical, but it made an impact on me. And I shared it with a lot of my Catholic friends.

Let's face it, anti-Catholicism can be a very reasonable thing. If the wafer Catholics worship is not Christ (and I was convinced it was not), then it is idolatrous and blasphemous to do what Catholics do in bowing before and worshiping the Eucharist. I was convinced of this, and I did my level best to share this. Please understand, my ardent anti-Catholicism sprang from a zeal for God and a charitable desire to help Catholics be Christians. And it was the Catholics who could outdrink and outswear me before I became a Christian, so I knew how much help they needed.

I was dating a Catholic at the time. I shared with her what is considered to be the bible of anti-Catholicism—a book I now believe to be filled with misrepresentations and lies about the Church—entitled *Roman Catholicism*, by Lorraine Boettner. My girlfriend read it and later wrote me a note thanking me for it, saying she'd never go back to Mass again. I later gave away copies to many other friends. I thanked God I could be used in that way, in all sincerity and blindness.

Grandma Hahn was the only Catholic on either side of the family. She was a quiet, humble and holy soul. Since I was the only "religious one" in the family, my father gave me her religious articles when she died. I looked at them with disgust and horror. I held her Rosary in my hands and ripped it apart, saying, "God, set her free from the chains of Catholicism that have bound her." I also tore apart her prayer books and threw them away, hoping this superstitious nonsense had not trapped her soul. I had been trained to regard this as excess baggage that humans invented to complicate a very simple, saving gospel. (I am not proud of having done these things, but I share them to point out how deeply and sincerely Bible Christians hold their anti–Catholic convictions.) I wasn't anti-Catholic in a bigoted way—I was anti-Catholic by conviction.

One episode reinforced this. At the end of my senior year I was on my way to the high school for a rehearsal when I passed the home of my former best friend, Dave. His light was on and I thought, I ought to stop by and at least say good-bye before graduating and going off to college. I had barely seen him in the past couple of years.

I rang the doorbell, and Dave's mom answered the door, inviting me in. I think she'd heard I'd gotten religion—she was so delighted to see me. As I stepped in, Dave was coming down the steps, putting his coat on. When he saw me, he stopped dead in his tracks. "Scott!?"

"Dave?"

"Come on up."

At first it was very awkward. Then we began to talk and talk. We were laughing and sharing, just like old times. What seemed like fifteen minutes ended up being over two hours. I completely missed my rehearsal! As I lamented this fact, I suddenly said, "But wait. You had your coat on. I'm sorry. I must have kept you from some plan, too."

Suddenly his whole complexion changed. "Why'd you come here tonight?"

"Just to say good-bye and have a nice life."

"But why tonight?"

"I don't know. Hey, did I make you miss something important?"

I looked at this big hunk of a guy who'd been so athletic, funny and popular, and his voice was shaking. "When you came, I was getting ready to go. . . ." He reached into his pocket and pulled out eight feet of rope, a noose at one end. "I was going out to hang myself. I was up in a tree in the old apple orchard this afternoon, getting ready to do it, and two little girls walked by. But I thought, I've already ruined my life, why ruin theirs? So I decided to do it tonight after it got dark. I was on my way out when you came."

He started to cry and asked me to pray for him. We embraced and I prayed for him right then and there. On the way out of his house, I noticed the crucifix hanging on the wall by the front door. I thought to myself: What a pity he's never heard the gospel. Stepping outside to walk home, I looked up to the stars and said to God, "Lord, I didn't know what he was about to do, but you did, didn't you? If you can use the likes of me to help a guy like Dave. . . . Here I am. Use me some more— especially to help Catholics."

Kimberly:

Just before Christmas bells rang in 1957, my father was given the news that his firstborn child was born: Kimberly Lorraine. His heart rejoiced with my mother.

My parents, Jerry and Patricia Kirk, bathed me in prayer from the first moment they knew I was on the way right up to the present day. They fed me the Word of God right along with my peas and potatoes. They baptized me as a baby and taught me the faith from my earliest moments. They set a good example, always learning about the Lord and growing in their faith life. And their love for each other and the Lord provided a tremendous foundation for my faith. What a rich heritage!

Along with the psalmist they could say, "I will sing of the steadfast love of the Lord, thy mercy, O Lord, forever. With my mouth I will proclaim thy faithfulness to all generations" (Ps 89:1).

Because I loved my parents, I loved the God they loved. Because I believed my parents, I believed in the God they believed in—that he had done what they said he had done. I believed the Bible was true because they said it was. And yet there comes a time when each of us needs to decide about whether or not Jesus' claims on our lives are, in fact, true.

One day in seventh grade I had that opportunity to make it my own. Raised in a solid Christian family, I was one of those typically "good" kids who don't do a lot of big, external sins as much as sins in attitudes and thoughts. The sins of omission tended to be greater than the sins of commission. But that day I was very conscious of how much I was failing God, and I was primed to listen to Dr. Lloyd Ogilvie preach.

I heard the gospel in a way that convicted my heart: God loved me and had a desire for me to live with and for him, but my own sins separated me from him and those sins had to be forgiven for me to be close to God. That was why Jesus had come. I had to acknowledge my own need. I had to ask specifically for forgiveness for those sins—saying, "Jesus, be my Savior." And I had to say to him, "I want you on the throne of my life—Jesus, be my Lord." No longer held by the hand of my parents, I needed to be grasped firmly by the hand of my heavenly Father.

The preacher had barely finished the "altar call" before I was running down the steps of the balcony and up the aisle to say, "Yes, Jesus. Yes, I need you. Yes, I want you to be at the center of my life."

Psalm 51:1 says, "Have mercy on me, O God, according to thy steadfast love, according to thy steadfast mercies, blot out my transgressions." That was my prayer.

This experience plunged me into an entirely new relationship with the Lord. I had a desire to learn about my faith as never before. I wanted to fast—not because I was being told to, but because I wanted more of God than before. I had a hunger for the Word of God, to read it, to study it and to memorize it. And I looked forward to confirmation later that year, not only to share my faith with the elders of our church, but also to begin receiving communion. When I thought of approaching the table of the Lord, I related it to the experience my mother had provided me day after day at supper: it was homecoming after the battles of the day; it was a celebration of one another; it was a love feast served with beauty and grace. Little did I know how much more she prepared my heart for future reception of the Eucharist than for Presbyterian communion.

I had chances to live my faith in new ways: witnessing constantly, carrying my Bible on the top of my books to read as well as to spawn conversations (which it did), helping start prayer groups in the morning before classes. . . . I was obnoxious, at times. But converts can be that way—and they tend to be more fruitful many times than those staid and steadyhanded in the faith.

I grew in love—letting God love me just the way I was, loving God in new ways and learning how to treat my brothers and sisters in Christ. My junior- and senior-high years were filled with all kinds of exciting ministries: leading Bible studies, evangelizing and singing with a Christian teen group called Young Folk, as we led worship services in local churches and on summer tours. This helped to establish a strong, Christian peer group for me.

I had difficult but invigorating battles at my public high school. I would share my faith and get challenged by students and teachers. Then I would come home and my parents would fortify me, giving me more Scripture to take back. I seemed to be living up to my name— Kimberly means "warrior maiden" in Gaelic. I really enjoyed those confrontations, I must say. I was curious to see if a Christian college would have as many challenges.

The Kirk family, 1962. Kimberly is sitting on her mother's lap.

May, 1979. Graduation Day. Grove City College, Grove City, Pennsylvania.

2

From Ministry to Marriage

Scott:

The summer before going off to college, I toured the United States, Scotland, England and Holland, playing guitar in a Christian musical group, the Continentals. By the end, I got the guitar and music out of my system enough to want to concentrate on Scripture and theology in college.

My four years at Grove City College went by in a whirlwind. I majored in theology, philosophy and economics—I added the last one to satisfy my more practical father, who was paying the tuition bills. I also got involved in the local branch of Young Life. I wanted to return the favor to God for using Young Life to introduce me to the gospel. So I worked in that organization all four years, evangelizing and discipling high-school kids in the faith, as I had received it.

I'd like to relate a story that captures the zeal that motivated me in sharing the gospel with people who didn't know Christ.

An acquaintance told me about Dr. Francis Schaeffer, a great Christian scholar with whom he was studying in Europe. Dr. Schaeffer decided to take a weekend off to visit Paris with a couple of his students. One night as they strolled the streets of Paris, they saw a prostitute on a street corner. To the students' horror, they watched their mentor walk right up to the woman.

He said, "How much do you charge?"

"Fifty dollars."

He eyed her up and down and said, "Nah, that's too little."

"Oh yeah, for Americans, it's one hundred fifty dollars."

He stepped back again, "That's still too low."

She quickly said, "Uhh, oh yeah, the weekend rate for Americans is five hundred dollars."

"No, that's still too cheap."

By this time she was a little irritated. She said, "What am I worth to you?"

He responded, "Lady, I couldn't possibly pay you what you are worth, but let me tell you about someone who already has."

The two men watched as their mentor—right then and there—knelt with her on the sidewalk and led her in a prayer to commit her life to Christ.

That's the kind of zeal to share the gospel that we had in Young Life; and for the life of me I couldn't understand why so many mainstream churches didn't even seem to care.

I deliberately targeted Roman Catholics out of compassion and concern for their errors and superstitions. When it came to leading Bible studies for the high-school kids, I strategically aimed my teachings to reach Catholic young people, who I felt were so lost and confused. I was especially alarmed at their ignorance—not only of the Bible but of their own Church's teachings. For some reason, they didn't even know the basics of the catechism. I got the feeling that they were being treated like guinea pigs in their own CCD programs. As a result, getting them to see their Church's "errors" was like shooting ducks in a barrel.

Back in the dorm, some of my friends began talking about getting "rebaptized". We were all growing fast in the faith together and attending a local fellowship. The minister—a spellbinding speaker—was teaching that those of us who were baptized as babies were never *really* baptized. My friends seemed to go along with everything he said. The next day they were sitting down to agree on a date for getting "dunked for real".

I spoke up. "Don't you think we ought to study the Bible for ourselves to make sure he's right?"

They didn't seem to hear. "What's wrong with what he's saying, Scott? After all, do you remember getting baptized? What good is baptism for babies, who can't believe anyway?"

I wasn't really sure myself. But I knew the answer wasn't to play "follow the leader"—to base my beliefs simply on feelings, as they seemed to be doing. So I told them, "I don't know about you, but I'm going to study the Bible some more before rushing into rebaptism."

Next week they got "rebaptized".

Meanwhile, I went to one of my Bible professors and told him what was happening. He wouldn't tell me his opinion. Instead, he urged me to study the issue more closely. "Scott, why not make infant baptism the topic for your research paper in my class?"

I was stuck.

To be honest, I didn't want to study it *that* much. But I guess the Lord knew I needed a little extra pressure. So for the next few months I read everything I could get my hands on.

By this point in my Christian life, I had already read through the Bible three or four times. From my reading, I was convinced that the key to understanding the Bible was the idea of the covenant. It's there on every page—with God making one in every age!

Studying the covenant made one thing clear. For two thousand years, from the time of Abraham to the coming of Christ, God showed his people that he wanted their babies to be in covenant with him. The way to do it was simple: give them the sign of the covenant.

Of course, back in the Old Testament, the sign of entering God's covenant was circumcision; whereas Christ changed it to baptism in the New Testament. But nowhere did I find Christ announcing that, from now on, babies were to be kept out of the covenant.

In fact, I found him saying practically the opposite: "Let the children come to me, and do not hinder them; for to such belongs the kingdom of heaven" (Mt 19:14).

I also found the apostles imitating him. For example, at Pentecost, when Peter finished his first sermon, he called everyone to embrace Christ by entering into the New Covenant: "Repent and be baptized every one of you in the name of Jesus Christ for the forgiveness of your sins; and you shall receive the gift of the Holy Spirit. For the promise is to you *and to your children . . .*" (Acts 2:38–39).

In other words, God still wanted children in covenant with him. And since the New Testament gave only baptism as the sign for entering the New Covenant, why should the babies of believers not be baptized? No wonder, as I discovered in my study, the Church practiced infant baptism from the beginning.

I went to my friends with the results of my biblical research. They didn't want to hear it—much less discuss it. In fact, I sensed that they felt uncomfortable with my even studying the issue.

I made two discoveries that day. For one thing, I learned that many so-called Bible Christians prefer to base their beliefs on feelings, without praying and thinking through Scripture. For another, I discovered that the covenant was *really* the key for unlocking the whole Bible.

I decided then, my freshman year, that the covenant would be the focus of my study for all future class papers and projects. And I followed through on it. In fact, after four years of studying the covenant, I determined that it was really the overarching theme of the entire Bible. Scripture was making more and more sense.

By my senior year at college, I had one other goal besides going to seminary for graduate studies in Scripture and theology: to marry the most beautiful and spiritual woman on campus, Miss Kimberly Kirk.

I had already recruited her as a Young Life leader. For two years, we ministered side by side. Then I proposed marriage to her. To my delight, she accepted.

After I graduated from college with highest honors in theology and philosophy, I moved to Cincinnati so that we could spend the summer preparing for marriage. With Kimberly Hahn at my side, I was ready to face the future, full steam ahead.

Kimberly:

I enrolled at Grove City College in 1975 to begin my undergraduate degree in Communication Arts. I had chosen a Christian college, not to get a break from the battles that had really invigorated my walk with God back in a secular, public high school, but to grow in a more deeply challenging way: to be iron sharpening iron with other

Christians. However, once in college, the dilemma in which I found myself floundering was the ease with which I could slough off growing in a dynamic way, because most people either were Christians or acted like it. I wasn't going forward in my relationship to Christ; this meant I was going backward, since it wasn't possible to stand still.

The summer between my sophomore and junior years I was convicted about my spiritual slump at college. I'd had a great time being in plays, a sorority and clubs, but I really hadn't grown spiritually. Jesus was not asking to be at the center of my life—he was requiring it. I knew that, but I was acting as though I had invited him into my life on my terms, when it was convenient for me. However, he was the One inviting me into his life. I needed to find a ministry that would really drive me to my knees, something that was simply too big for me to conquer on my own. I was at that place of a fresh yielding to the Lord when I returned to Grove City College for my junior year.

When I came back in the fall I was involved in the Orientation Board, and Scott was a Resident Assistant. For these reasons we were both involved in the freshman dance. I noticed him at the dance, and I thought, He's too handsome to go over and talk to. Then I thought, No, he isn't. I can go and talk to him.

So I went over and started talking to him. Almost immediately he said to me, "Do you believe God exists?"

I thought, Oh, Lord, this guy has lost his faith over the summer. Give me the words to say. For ten minutes I stumbled through my explanation that God does, in fact, exist. I finally said, "Do you think God exists?"

And he said, "Oh, yeah."

Surprised, I said, "Why have you been drilling me for the last ten minutes?"

"I wanted to see what you were made of", was his reply. "Do you want to take a walk?"

So we went for a walk.

I shared my conviction from the summer that the last two years in college would differ from the first two by my involvement in some kind of ministry that would challenge me to grow spiritually. "Have I got the ministry for you!" Scott announced. "Have you ever heard of Young Life?"

I knew about Young Life because my father had come to faith in Christ through Young Life in Colorado. When Dad attended seminary in Pittsburgh, he had brought the ministry of Young Life into the Pittsburgh area. What I didn't know was that it was Pittsburgh's Young Life ministry that had reached Scott for Christ. After that experience, he had come to college to be involved in the local high-school Young Life club and was really interested in recruiting strong girl leaders to help him.

Scott described it. "We go up to the high school and we hang out. We get to know the kids. We go to their games, give them rides home from school and love them right where they are. We win the right to be heard, and, at the right time, we share Christ with them. Then we disciple the kids who have committed their lives to Christ. We challenge them down to their toenails on what it means to live for Christ. I need girl leaders. Will you come on board?"

I knew it was something that would really demand getting on my knees. I was scared to death! So I said, "All right. That's what I'm supposed to do."

For the next two years, we served in the Young Life

ministry with some other college students, side by side. At first, it was scary to go to the high school just to hang out, but we wanted to become friends with the students to share the Lord with them. God was really with us, strengthening us; the fruit was abundant.

Scott taught the leaders effective ways of communicating the gospel and discipling. He played the guitar for the music and gave many of the talks at our weekly club meetings. He led such challenging Bible studies for the kids that all the leaders wanted to attend. In fact, he had to discourage some leaders from coming because the room was so crowded with students.

Scott and I spent some extra time together just after he recruited me. We would begin talking at lunch and finish just after supper. After about three weeks of some rather intense sharing times, Scott said, "Kimberly, I'm really enjoying our time together. But if we spend more of this kind of time, I'm going to fall in love with you. And I don't have time this year to fall in love. Maybe next year. I think we should stop dating."

I was really surprised. That sure was a creative way to break up. I was disappointed, to be sure. But I felt he was the godliest man I had ever dated, so I took him at his word that there wasn't some other hidden reason he was ending things. We backed out of our dating but continued to serve in ministry together.

Young Life seemed to fit into my plans to be trained to be a minister, a dream I had had since I was in second grade. My dad convinced me by his life that being a pastor was the most exciting job in the world. He came home day after day, thrilled with sharing the gospel so that people could come to faith in Christ, counseling couples in marital difficulty and seeing their marriages restored, teaching and preaching the Word of God and bringing comfort to those grappling with sickness and death. Nothing seemed more wonderful than imitating him in the call of pastoring. I believed I had many of the same gifts and talents he had, similar abilities, drives and desires to share the gospel and disciple others for Jesus Christ.

Then some good friends, including Scott, began to challenge me during my junior year, from Scripture, on whether or not God was, in fact, calling me to be a minister. I agreed with them that if the Scriptures did not support it, then God had a different plan for my life.

It was very difficult to examine a dream that had been mine for so long and to alter that dream. But I had to, once I became convicted that Scripture did not support the ordination of women to be pastors. However, once that became my conviction, my deep desire to be ordained diminished, and I looked for another way the Lord would use my talents and desire to serve him.

Besides being very involved in Young Life, Scott and I also enjoyed bantering over theology, sometimes in rather strong discussions. At Christmas my junior year, I was at home describing one of these conversations to my mother, and she said, "Why, Kimberly, I wonder if you won't marry this guy. I'll bet you do."

"Marry him! I can hardly have a theological conversation with him without getting frustrated!"

"Yes, I think you'll probably marry him." She had never said that about any other guy I had ever dated. I noted her words.

Though we were not dating any more, Scott and I built a great foundation for a future dating relationship. Unbeknownst to me, Scott told people the summer before our senior year that he intended to return to

college and to date and marry Kimberly Kirk. Toward
the end of summer, I too had a deep sense that he was
the one for me.

On September 31, during a Young Life leadership training weekend, we began to date again. Through our
Young Life ministry together, we saw how much family
life could prosper through ministry, like two oxen pulling
as a team. I appreciated Scott's drive for the truth and his
love for the Word. He was a powerful communicator.
Lives changed as the Lord worked through him. And Scott
appreciated who I was and how the Lord used me as well.

Scott and I again had long talks—sharing what we had
been thinking and studying. We had very complementary
dreams. He wanted to be a minister and a teacher; I
wanted to be a pastor's wife. He wanted to be a writer; I
enjoyed typing and editing. Both of us liked to speak.
Even though we wrangled over theology, we had tremendous unity theologically, and that let us know that,
holding such similar convictions, we could go forward
together stronger being side by side than we could in our
own individual ways.

By January 23 we were engaged to be wed the following August. (Our engagement date, we have recently discovered, is the Stigmatine Fathers' feast day of the
betrothal of Mary and Joseph!) Shortly before graduation,
I realized I did not know whether or not he wanted a
large family. I had always hoped that I could have at least
four or five children. So I casually brought it up, saying,
"You do want children, don't you?"

"Well, not too many."

I thought, Oh, no, he's a ZPGer (Zero Population
Growth advocate)! Still trying to sound casual, I said,
"How many is not too many?"

"I don't know", he said. "I think we ought to keep it down to five or six."

I could hardly believe my ears. "Yeah, let's think small", I said with a smile.

This was just one more way our hearts and minds were united. Each of us was amazed at the gift that God had given the other. And to think the differences in our theology were basically resolved! All we had to do was get married, go off to seminary and explore the truth we found there. Then we would set off to conquer the world for Jesus Christ. At least that's what we thought.

On August 18, 1979, in Cincinnati, before our families and more than five hundred friends, we covenanted ourselves in marriage to have Jesus be the center of our life together. We had enough dreams to last a lifetime.

Scott and Kimberly's wedding. August 18, 1979 in Cincinnati, Ohio.

Married life in the seminary. September, 1981.

3

New Conceptions of the Covenant

Scott:

Kimberly and I arrived at Gordon-Conwell Theological Seminary just two weeks after our wedding. We were both firmly convinced that evangelical, reformed theology was biblical Christianity at its best.

At this point I would describe my study as a *detective* story. I was searching Scripture to discover clues as to the whereabouts of real Christianity: Where was the Bible being faithfully taught and lived out? Wherever that was, I knew God wanted me there—for a lifetime of teaching. I was an energetic detective, willing to follow Scripture no matter what it taught.

I met a fellow seminarian named Gerry Matatics, who quickly became a close friend. (He figures large in the story later.) Among the Presbyterian students, we were the only ones stalwart enough in our anti-Catholicism to believe the Westminster Confession ought to retain a line most reformed people were willing to drop: the Pope is the Antichrist. Although the Reformers—Luther, Calvin, Zwingli, Knox and others—disagreed on many things, one conviction they all shared was that the Pope was the Antichrist and that the Church of Rome was the whore of Babylon.

When the Pope came to Boston in 1979, many fellow seminarians said, "Isn't he wonderful?" Wonderful! He claimed the power to bind hundreds of millions of hearts and minds as the supposedly infallible teacher of the universe. That's wonderful? That's abominable! Gerry and I worked in the seminary to help our brethren see just how wrong it was.

My second year of seminary was Kimberly's first. Something very curious occurred when she took a course on Christian ethics. I had taken this course previously, so I knew the class would divide into small groups to work on a single moral issue. I asked Kimberly what topic she had chosen.

She said, "Contraception."

"Contraception?! That was an option last year, but nobody took it. It's really just a Catholic problem. Why would you want to study contraception?"

"I keep running into questions about birth control when I give talks on abortion. I don't know why, but I do. So I thought this would be a good chance to find out whether or not the Bible has anything to say about it."

"Well, if you want to waste your time studying a non-issue, it's your time." I was surprised but not really concerned. After all, there really wasn't a right or wrong way to look at contraception. Little did I know how much her study would affect our lives.

A couple of weeks later a friend stopped me in the hall. "Have you talked to your wife about her study on contraception?"

"Not really."

"You might want to. She's come up with some pretty interesting thoughts about it."

Given the subject matter, I thought I'd better talk to her. I asked Kimberly what she had found out that was so interesting about contraception. She shared that before

1930 there had been a unified witness of all Christian churches: contraception was wrong in all circumstances.

I conjectured, "Maybe it's taken this long to work out the last vestiges of Catholicism."

She challenged me further. "But do you know what reasons they give to oppose birth control? They have stronger reasons than you might think."

I had to admit I didn't know their reasons. She asked me if I would read a book on the subject. She handed me *Birth Control and the Marriage Covenant*, by John Kippley (which has since been revised and retitled *Sex and the Marriage Covenant*). I was a specialist in covenant theology. I thought I owned all the books that had the word "covenant" in the title, so this piqued my curiosity.

I looked at it and thought, Liturgical Press? This guy's a Catholic! A Papist! What was he doing hijacking the Protestant notion of the covenant? I was curious to see what he would say. I sat down to read the book. I thought, This isn't right—it can't be! This man is making sense. He was showing how marriage is not a contract, involving merely an exchange of goods and services. Rather, marriage is a covenant, involving an exchange of persons.

Kippley's argument was that every covenant has an act whereby the covenant is enacted and renewed; and that the marital act is a covenant act. When the marriage covenant is renewed, God uses it to give new life. To renew the marital covenant and use birth control to destroy the potential for new life is tantamount to receiving the Eucharist and spitting it on the ground.

Kippley showed that the marital act demonstrates the powerful life-giving love of the covenant in a unique way. All the other covenants show God's love and trans-

mit God's love, but it is only in the marital covenant that
the love is so real and powerful that it communicates life.

When God made man, male and female, the first command he gave them was to be fruitful and multiply. This
was to image God—Father, Son and Holy Spirit, three in
one, the Divine Family. So when "the two become one"
in the covenant of marriage, the "one" they become is so
real that nine months later they might have to give it a
name! The child embodies their covenant oneness.

I began to see that every time Kimberly and I per-
formed the marital act we were doing something sacred.
And every time we thwarted the life-giving power of
love through contraception, we were doing something
profane. (Treating something sacred in a merely common
way profanes it, by definition.)

I was impressed, but I was very quiet about being impressed. Kimberly asked me what I thought of the book;
I said it was interesting. Then I began to watch her pick
off my friends, one at a time—some of the best and the
brightest changed their minds!

Then I discovered how all the reformers—Luther, Calvin, Zwingli, Knox, and all the rest—held the same position as the Catholic Church on this issue.

I grew disturbed. The Roman Catholic Church stood
alone as the only "denomination" in all the world with
the courage and integrity to teach this most unpopular
truth. I did not know what to make of it. So I resorted to
an old family saying: "Even a blind hog can find an
acorn." I mean, after two thousand years, the Catholic
Church was bound to get something right.

Catholic or not, it was true. So we threw out the con-
traceptives we were using and began trusting the Lord in
a new way with our family plans. First, we used Natural

Family Planning for a number of months. Then we decided to be open to new life whenever God saw fit to bless us.

I organized a cadre of a dozen of the top Calvinist seminarians at Gordon-Conwell into a weekly breakfast group to talk about issues, inviting professors to share their views and be cross-examined. It was a great time of fellowship and stimulating conversation. We called it the Geneva Academy, after Calvin's school in Geneva.

Sometimes we would get together on Friday nights, meeting at Howard Johnson's or some local pub for pizza and beer in order to talk theology until three in the morning, with a promise to our wives to take them out the next night. For three or four hours we would go deeper into the Word of God, debating hard doctrines: Christ's second coming, arguments for God's existence, predestination and free will and other great mysteries that theologians love to explore, especially the covenant.

Digging deeper into Scripture meant wrestling more and more with the meaning of key texts on our own. We were acquiring some skills in Greek and Hebrew. For us, the Bible alone was our authority; therefore, having these skills meant that we could go straight into Scripture. For us, no traditions were infallible or authoritative. They might be helpful. They might be reliable. But they were not infallible; so they might slip and slide and fall at any point. In practice, this required all of us as individuals to rethink doctrine from the ground up. It was quite a task, but we were young, and so we believed that with the Holy Spirit and Sacred Scripture we could reinvent all the wheels, if need be.

In my senior year, a crisis began brewing. My research was forcing me to rethink the meaning of the covenant.

In the Protestant tradition, covenants and contracts were understood as two words describing the same thing. But studying the Old Testament led me to see that, for the ancient Hebrews, covenants and contracts were very different. In Scripture, contracts simply involved the exchange of property, whereas covenants involved the exchange of persons, so as to form sacred family bonds. Kinship was thus formed by covenant. (Understood from its Old Testament background, the concept of covenant wasn't theoretical or abstract.) In fact, covenant kinship was stronger than biological kinship; the deeper meaning of divine covenants in the Old Testament was God's fathering of Israel as his own family.

When Christ formed the New Covenant with us, then, it was much more than a simple contract or legal exchange, where he took our sin and gave us his righteousness, as Luther and Calvin explained it. Although true, that explanation fell short of the full truth of the gospel.

What I discovered was that the New Covenant established a new worldwide family in which Christ shared his own divine sonship, making us children of God. As a covenant act, being justified meant sharing in the grace of Christ as God's sons and daughters; being sanctified meant sharing in the life and power of the Holy Spirit. In this light, God's grace became something much more than divine favor; it was the actual gift of God's life in divine sonship.

Luther and Calvin explained this exclusively in terms of courtroom language. But I was beginning to see that, far more than simply being a judge, God was our Father. Far more than simply being criminals, we were runaways. Far more than the New Covenant being made in a courtroom, it was fashioned by God in a family room.

Saint Paul (whom I had thought of as the first Luther) taught in Romans, Galatians and elsewhere that justification was more than a legal decree; it established us in Christ as God's children by grace alone. In fact, I discovered that nowhere did Saint Paul ever teach that we were justified by faith *alone*! *Sola fide* was unscriptural!

I was so excited about this discovery. I shared it with some friends, who were amazed at how much sense it made. Then one friend stopped me and asked if I knew who else was teaching this way on justification. When I responded that I didn't, he told me that Dr. Norman Shepherd, a professor at Westminster Theological Seminary (the strictest Presbyterian Calvinist seminary in America) was about to undergo a heresy trial for teaching the same view of justification that I was expounding.

So I called Professor Shepherd and talked with him. He said he was accused of teaching something contrary to the teachings of Scripture, Luther and Calvin. As I heard him describe what he was teaching, I thought, Hey, that *is* what I'm saying.

Now this might not seem like much of a crisis to many, but for somebody steeped in Protestantism and convinced that Christianity turned on the hinge of *sola fide*, it meant the world.

I remembered how one of my favorite theologians, Dr. Gerstner, once said in class that if Protestants were wrong on *sola fide*—and the Catholic Church was right that justification is by faith *and* works—"I'd be on my knees tomorrow morning outside of the Vatican doing penance." We all knew, of course, that he said that for rhetorical effect, but it made a real impact. In fact, the whole Reformation flowed from this one difference.

Luther and Calvin often said that this was the article on which the Church stood or fell. That was why, for them, the Catholic Church fell and Protestantism rose up from the ashes. *Sola fide* was the material principle of the Reformation, and I was coming to the conviction that Saint Paul never taught it.

In James 2:24, the Bible teaches that "a man is justified by works and not by faith alone." Besides, Saint Paul said in 1 Corinthians 13:2, ". . . if I have all faith so as to remove mountains, but have not love, I am nothing." This was a traumatic transformation for me to say that on this point I now thought Luther was fundamentally wrong. For seven years, Luther had been my main source of inspiration and powerful proclamation of the Word. And this doctrine had been the rationale behind the whole Protestant Reformation.

At this point, I put my investigation on hold. Kimberly and I were planning for me to pursue doctoral studies at the University of Aberdeen, Scotland, where I had been accepted as a candidate for the degree, focusing on the covenant; that is, until we discovered, much to our delight, that the Lord had blessed our openness to new life with our first child. A change in our theology had produced a change in Kimberly's anatomy. But at the time, Margaret Thatcher made it almost impossible for Americans to have babies at British taxpayers' expense; so we took this as a sign for us to look elsewhere for work, delaying doctoral studies for a while.

We got a call from a small church in Fairfax, Virginia, that was looking for a minister. When I candidated for the position at Trinity Presbyterian Church, I shared my views and concerns regarding justification—that I took Dr. Shepherd's position. They understood and said they did, too. So, shortly before graduation, I accepted the pastorate at Trinity, as well as a teaching position in their high school, Fairfax Christian School.

By God's grace, I found myself graduating at the top of my class. It was time to say good-bye to some of the finest friends I'd ever made—both students and professors. God had blessed us with very deep friendships with men and women who were really serious about opening up their minds and hearts to the Word of God. Kimberly and I graduated together; she earned a Master of Arts degree in theology, while I received a Master of Divinity degree.

Kimberly:

Our first year in seminary Scott began his Master's degree studying the fine points of theology with professors who had been teaching theology for ten to forty years. Meanwhile, I was a secretary for a program funded by a Harvard research grant, working with people who were every kind of religion but Christian, many of whom had never heard the gospel and had never read the Bible at all. They challenged me almost daily as to whether or not God even existed. It was quite a contrast.

After the first year, we decided to get on the same track and grow together. So, with Scott's blessing and my parents' assistance, I began my Master's studies during Scott's second year. It was a rich experience to study theology side by side.

One of the first issues I tackled in a course on Christian ethics was contraception. I had not thought it was an issue to be studied until I became involved in pro-life work. For some reason, birth control kept creeping in as an issue. Being a Protestant, I did not know any friends who did not practice birth control. I'd been counseled to practice birth control as reasonable, responsible Christian behavior. In premarital counseling, we had been asked what kind of birth control we were going to use, not whether or not we were going to use it.

The small group focusing on "contraception" met in the back of the class briefly the first day. A self-appointed leader spoke up. "We don't have to consider the Catholic position because there are only two reasons Catholics oppose contraception. Number one, the Pope isn't married, so he doesn't have to live with the consequences. And number two, they just want all the Catholics they can have in the world."

"Are those the reasons the Catholic Church gives?" I interrupted. "I don't think so."

"Then why don't you study it?"

"I will." And I did.

First, I looked at the nature of God and how we as marriage partners are called to image him. God—Father, Son and Holy Spirit—made man and woman in his image and blessed them in the covenant of marriage with the command to be fruitful and multiply, filling the earth and having dominion over all of creation, to the glory of God (Gen 1:26–28). The very image in which man and woman were created was the unity of the three Persons of the Godhead, pouring themselves out in total self-donating love to each other. God restated this creation mandate in his covenant with Noah and his family with the same command to be fruitful and multiply (Gen 9:1ff.). So the existence of sin did not change the call of married couples to image God through procreation.

Saint Paul clarified that, in the New Covenant, marriage was elevated to the status of imaging the relationship between Christ and the Church. (At this point I had no idea that marriage was actually a sacrament.) And by the very life-giving power of love, God enabled a couple to reflect the image of God as the unity of the two became three. The question I asked myself was, Does our use of birth control—intentionally blocking the life-giving power of love while enjoying the unity and pleasure that the act of marriage gives us—enable my spouse and me to reflect the image of God in total self-donating love?

Second, I examined what Scripture had to say about children. The witness of the Word was overwhelming! Every verse that spoke about children spoke of them as only and always a blessing (Ps 127; 128). There was no proverb that cautioned about the expenses of a child outweighing his worth. There was no blessing pronounced over the man or woman who had perfect spacing between children, or the couple who had the right number of childless years before shouldering the burden of children, or the husband and wife who had planned each conception. These were thoughts I had learned from the media, my public school and my neighborhood, but they had no foundation in the Word of God.

Fertility, in Scripture, was presented as something to be prized and celebrated rather than as a disease to be avoided at all costs. And though I could find no verse speaking negatively about people with small families, there was no question that larger families showed an outpouring of greater favor from God, according to a variety of passages. God was the One who opened and closed the womb, and, when he gave life, it was seen only as a blessing. After all, God's desire from faithful marriages was "godly offspring" (Mal 2:15). Children were described as "arrows in the hand of a warrior . . . blessed is the man whose quiver is full." Who would go into battle with only two or three arrows when he could go with a whole quiver-full?! The question I asked myself was, Did our use of birth control reflect how God saw children or how the world saw children?

Third was the issue of the lordship of Jesus Christ. As evangelical Protestants, Scott and I took Christ's lordship over our lives very seriously. In terms of money, we tithed regularly no matter how tight funds were because we wanted to be good stewards of the money he had put in our care. Over and over we had seen the Lord meet our needs beyond what we had given to him. In terms of time, we honored the Lord's Day, setting aside our studies, which were our work, even if we had exams on Monday. Many times over, the Lord blessed us with that day off, and we aced every exam we took on Mondays. In terms of talents, we assumed that we should always be available to serve the Lord in ministry and added service to our study workload gladly. To see lives blessed as a result of that ministry strengthened our faith and our marriage greatly.

But our bodies? Our fertility? Did Christ's lordship extend that far? Then I read 1 Corinthians 6:19–20: "You are not your own. You were bought with a price. So glorify God in your bodies." Perhaps it was more of an American attitude than a godly one to think of our fertility as something for us to control as we deemed best. The question I asked myself was, Did our use of birth control demonstrate faithfully living out the lordship of Jesus Christ?

Fourth, what was the will of God for Scott and me? We wanted to know and to follow the will of God for our lives. One Scripture passage that provided helpful food for thought was Romans 12:1–2:

> I appeal to you, therefore, brethren, by the mercies of God to present your bodies as a living sacrifice, holy and acceptable to God which is your spiritual worship. Do not be conformed to this world but be transformed by the renewal of your minds, that you may prove what is the will of God, what is good and acceptable and perfect.

Paul pointed out that a sacrificial life required the mercy of God—we were not asked to live this kind of life in our own strength. We could offer our own bodies as a sacrifice in worship—there was a physical side to being spiritual. One of the keys to knowing how to sacrifice in a way that proved the will of God was to differentiate properly between the messages of the world and the truths of God. That meant we had to renew our minds actively in God's Word. And so much of my study in the area of contraception had led me to do just that— meditate on Scriptures that presented a different picture from what the world seemed to shout.

Scott and I were already committed to each other and to the Lord. The question was, Could God be trusted to plan the size of our family? the spacing of children? Would he know what we could handle financially, emotionally and spiritually? Did he have the resources to enable us to handle more children than we thought we could?

At root I knew what I was wrestling with—the very sovereignty of God. God alone knew the future and what would be the best way for us to build our family with the godly offspring that he so desired for us to have. He certainly had proven himself trustworthy in countless other ways. I knew we could trust him to provide the faith we needed to entrust this area of our lives to him, to give us the hope that this vision was a part of his plan for our lives and to pour out his love in and through us to whatever precious souls he would place in our care. And, after all, I knew many couples at our seminary who "planned" when babies were to come, only to find God's timing different from their own. We needed to trust in him in the area of our fertility in a radical way—without the use of birth control. Needless to say, I was convinced; but there were two people in our marriage, and I needed to raise these concerns and questions with Scott.

When Scott asked at supper one evening how my study on contraception was going, I shared as much as I could. Then I asked him to read the book by John Kippley entitled *Birth Control and the Marriage Covenant*. Scott saw the substance of my arguments in this book; but even more, he saw how Kippley applied the idea of covenant in marriage to explain why contraception was immoral.

Kippley gave the following comparison. Just as in ancient Rome, when people would feast and then excuse themselves to vomit the food they had just consumed (to avoid the consequences of their actions), so it is with spouses who feast in the act of marriage only to thwart the life-giving power of their act of covenant renewal. Both actions are contrary to natural law and the marital covenant.

From Kippley's perspective, representing the Catholic Church, the primary end or purpose of the marriage act is the procreation of children. When a couple intentionally thwarts that end, they are acting contrary to natural law.

They are subverting the renewal of their own marriage covenant, making a lie out of their commitment to give themselves totally to each other.

Now I understood why the Roman Catholic Church opposed contraception, but what about Natural Family Planning (NFP)? Wasn't this just Catholic birth control?

First Corinthians 7:4–5, speaks of periods of time in which spouses could abstain from sexual relations for reasons of prayer and then resume relations to keep Satan from getting a foothold in their marriage. In reading *Humanae Vitae*, I came to appreciate the balance of the Church in her understanding about contraception. There was a godly way to experience the act of marriage and to be prudent in serious circumstances by practicing continence during times of mutual fertility.

Just as with food, there could be times when fasting was helpful; so there could be times when fasting from the act of marriage for prayerfully considered reasons could be helpful. Yet, apart from a miracle, one could barely survive while fasting most of the time. So, likewise, NFP was presented as a prescription for difficulty rather than as a daily vitamin for general health.

One day in the library, after I had explained all of this to a fellow seminarian who was still single, he challenged me. "So, Kimberly, have you and Scott stopped using birth control?"

"No, not yet."

"You sure sound like you are convinced that it's wrong."

I responded with this story.

"Have you ever heard about the time Farmer Brown's chicken and pig were discussing how blessed they were with such a wonderful master?

" 'I think we should do something special for Farmer Brown', said the chicken.

" 'What do you have in mind?' asked the pig.

" 'Let's give him a ham-and-eggs breakfast', quipped the chicken.

" 'Well,' retorted the pig, 'that's fine for you. For you that's a donation. For me that's total commitment.'

"Terry, I'll take your challenge to heart, but it's a lot harder for me to risk obedience in this area than for you as a single man."

After he agreed to pray for Scott and me, we went our separate ways home. When Scott and I discussed it, he agreed that he, too, was convicted against contraception; however, he suggested that perhaps we could just put the contraceptive on the shelf, just in case we changed our minds. I felt that would be too much of a temptation to go back on our convictions. So together we threw the birth control out and began a new level of trusting God with our lives and our fertility.

During our years in seminary, Scott and I had many opportunities to study theology side by side, encouraging, exhorting and challenging each other as well as our friends. Small group Bible studies as couples were a great source of blessing. Church ministry involvement gave us a challenge to apply what we were learning. And lots of theological discussions with fellow classmates over meals in our apartment kept life lively.

When I was with other women seminarians, the discussion would often turn to what job each hoped to get following graduation. Not too many were very affirming when I explained what I wanted to do with my degree: If I did not become pregnant, I would be open to taking a position teaching theology and doing ministry alongside

Scott; if I did become pregnant, which I hoped would happen soon, I would use the knowledge I had gained to be more of a help to Scott, to teach our children and to lead women's Bible studies.

My parents (who were footing the bill for my tuition) understood this as my goal and were very supportive. They didn't care if I ever drew a paycheck from my Master's degree. They saw it as an opportunity to develop my gifts for the Lord and trusted that the Lord would show us how they were to be used.

For the most part, the theological study was not so much a challenge to what we believed (such as in the case of contraception) as much as it was a deepening in our understanding of and appreciation for the foundation that had already been laid in our lives, with one notable exception: whether or not it is valid to assert that we are justified by faith alone.

We gradually became convinced that Martin Luther let his theological convictions contradict the very Scripture that he supposedly chose to obey rather than the Catholic Church. He declared that a person is not justified by faith working in love, but rather he is justified by faith alone. He even went so far as to add the word "alone" after the word "justified" in his German translation of Romans 3:28 and called Saint James "an epistle of straw" because James 2:24 specifically states, ". . . for we are not justified by faith alone".

Again, oddly enough to us, the Catholic Church was in the right on a key point: justification meant being made a child of God and being called to live life as a faithful child of God through faith working in love. Ephesians 2:8–10 clarified that faith—which we must have—was a gift from God, not because of our works, so that no one could boast; and that faith enabled us to do the good works God had planned for us to do. At the same time faith was a gift from God and our obedient response to the mercy of God. Both Protestants and Catholics could agree that salvation was by grace alone.

At this point, I was not steeped in Reformation theology, so the change in how I viewed justification did not seem momentous. It was important to understand it, but I felt that everybody could agree that we are saved by grace alone through faith working in love. And if I had had enough time to explain why I believed this, none of my friends would have labeled me Catholic at the time. However, for Scott, this theological shift was really a seismic change that later had major implications for our life.

As we neared the end of our final year at Gordon-Conwell, we discovered that the Lord had (finally) blessed us with a child. Though it altered our plans to go to Scotland to study, we were delighted to know the will of God included this child in our lives. Now I knew that what I had developed in my heart and mind during seminary I could apply and teach to this young one I was carrying under my heart. I had the deepest sense of fulfillment in being able to move on in my marriage vocation into motherhood. Following graduation, Scott and I felt sent forth to do the will of God with the people to whom he had called us in Virginia.

4

Teaching and Living the Covenant
as Family

Scott:

I began a pastorate in Virginia, preaching every Sunday an average of forty-five minutes in addition to leading two weekly Bible studies. That's what the elders of the church requested. I began preaching through the New Testament Epistle to the Hebrews, for no other New Testament book stresses the idea of the covenant as much. The congregation I was pastoring got very excited about the idea of the covenant as God's family.

The more I studied, the more surprised I was with the results, because this epistle was considered by Protestants I knew, and with whom I agreed, to be the most anti-Catholic epistle in the New Testament. "Once and for all sacrifice" and other such terms in Hebrews led us to that conclusion.

I was steeped in the understanding that "if something is Roman (meaning Roman Catholic), it must be wrong." But in fact, I began to see how important liturgy was for the covenant, especially in Hebrews. Liturgy represented the way God fathered his covenant family and renewed his covenant on a regular basis. I was eager to share what I thought were novel, innovative insights.

I wanted to see people fired up about the Old Testament and its relationship to the New—the Old flowing into the New and the New Testament Church as the fulfillment, rather than the abandonment, of the Old. As I dug deeper in my study, a disturbing pattern began to emerge: the novel ideas I thought I had discovered had actually been anticipated by the early Church Fathers.

I was shaken up by this same experience over and over again. Was I merely reinventing the wheel? I began to wonder.

As I shared these "novel finds" about God's covenant family and the worship of his children, my parishioners grew excited. The elders even asked me to revise our liturgy. Our liturgy? I wondered. Episcopalians were the ones who spoke of "liturgy"; Presbyterians have the "Order of Worship"! But the elders had asked me to revise the liturgy to fit the biblical pattern, so I began to study it.

I came up with some questions: Why is our church so pastor-centered? Why is our worship service so sermon-centered? And why aren't my sermons really designed to prepare God's people to receive communion?

I had already shown my parishioners that the one and only place where Christ used the word "covenant" was when he instituted the Eucharist, or communion, as we called it. Yet we only took communion four times a year. At first, it sounded foreign to all of us, but I submitted the proposal of weekly communion to the ruling elders.

One of them questioned me, "Scott, don't you think that celebrating communion every week might make it too much of a routine? After all, familiarity might breed contempt."

"Dick, we've seen how communion represents the renewal of our covenant with Christ, right?"

"Right."

"Well, let me ask you this. Do you prefer to renew your marriage covenant with your wife only four times a year? After all, it might become mere routine, and familiarity might breed contempt."

He laughed heartily, "I get your point."

Weekly communion was unanimously approved. We even began referring to it as the Eucharist (*eucharistia*), borrowing from the usage of the New Testament Greek and the early Church.

Celebrating communion each week became the high point of our church's worship service. It also changed our life as a congregation. We started having a potluck lunch after the service for fellowship, to discuss the sermon and to share prayer concerns. We began to practice communion and to live it as well. It was exciting. It brought a real sense of worship and community.

Next I took my parishioners through the Gospel of John, and, much to my shock, I discovered that the Gospel was loaded with sacramental imagery.

During my study, I recalled a conversation I had had a couple of years before in seminary with a good friend. He came up to my wife and me one morning in the hall, and he said, "I have been studying liturgy. It's exciting!"

I remembered my response to George. "Nothing bores me as much as liturgy except sacraments." That's the way I was in seminary because liturgy and the sacraments were not the things we studied. They weren't in our background; they weren't what we read in the text; they weren't things we were open to. But going through the Letter to the Hebrews and the Gospel of John made me see that liturgy and sacraments were an essential part of God's family life.

At this point, the detective story gradually became a *horror* story. All of a sudden, the Roman Catholic Church that I opposed seemed to be coming up with the right answer on one thing after another, much to my shock and dismay. After a number of instances, it got to be chilling.

During the week, I was teaching Scripture at a private Christian high school. I was sharing all about the covenant as the family of God, and my students were eating it up. I explained the series of covenants that God had established with his people.

I drew a time-line and showed how each covenant that God made was the way he went about fathering his family down through the ages. His covenant with Adam was a marriage; the covenant with Noah was a household; the covenant with Abraham was a tribe; the covenant with Moses made the twelve tribes into a national family; the covenant with David established Israel as a national kingdom family; while Christ made the New Covenant to be God's worldwide or "catholic" (from the Greek, *katholikos*) family to include all nations, both Jews and Gentiles.

They were so excited—it made sense out of the whole Bible.

One student asked, "What would this worldwide family look like?"

I drew a big pyramid on the board, explaining, "It would be like an extended family that covers the world, with different father figures at every level appointed by God to administer his love and his law to his children."

One of my Catholic students commented out loud, "That pyramid looks a lot like the Catholic Church, with the Pope at the top."

"Oh, no", I quickly replied. "What I'm giving you is the antidote to Catholicism." I really believed that, or at least I was trying to. "Besides, the Pope is a dictator; he's not a father."

"But Pope means father."

"No, it doesn't", I was quick to correct.

"Yes, it does", a number of students chorused.

Okay, so the Catholics got another thing right. I could admit it, though I was scared. Little did I know what was to follow.

At lunch one of my sharper students came up to me. Representing a little cadre of students in the back corner, she announced, "We took a vote, and it's unanimous: We think you're going to become a Roman Catholic."

I laughed—rather nervously. "That's crazy!" Chills ran up and down my spine. She smiled ever so smugly, folded her arms and went back to her seat.

I was still stunned when I arrived home later that afternoon. I said to Kimberly, "You'll never guess what Rebekah said today. She announced that a group of students took a vote and agreed that I'm going to become a Roman Catholic. Can you imagine anything so absurd?"

I waited for Kimberly to laugh with me. She just looked at me dead-pan and said, "Well, are you?"

I could not believe my ears! How could she think that I would betray the truth of Scripture and the Reformation with such ease? It felt like a dagger was being plunged into my back.

I stammered, "How can *you* say that? What a betrayal of your confidence in me as a pastor and a teacher. Catholic?! I was weaned on the writings of Martin Luther. What do you mean?"

"I used to think of you as very anti-Catholic and committed to the principles of the Reformation. But lately you're talking so much about sacraments, liturgy, typology and Eucharist."

Then she added something I'll never forget. "Sometimes I think you might be Luther in reverse."

Luther in reverse! I couldn't say anything. I went into my study, locked the door, slunk down into my desk chair, shaking. Luther in reverse? I was dazed, bewildered and confused. I could be losing my soul! I could be losing the gospel! I had always wanted to be a slave to the Word of God—and I believed I was. But where was it leading me? Luther in reverse—the words kept reverberating in my brain.

It was no longer merely theological speculation. Just weeks before, Kimberly had given birth to our son, Michael. I'll never forget the feeling of becoming a father for the first time. I looked at my child and realized that the life-giving power of the covenant was more than a theory.

As I held him in my arms, I wondered, to what church will he belong, or his children and grandchildren? After all, I was pastoring a Presbyterian church that had split off from a splinter group (the Orthodox Presbyterian Church), which had in turn separated from another division (the Presbyterian Church of the U.S.A.), all in this century! (We didn't call ourselves the split P's for nothing!)

Raising my own family created within me a longing for the unity of God's family, deeper than I had ever known before. For the sake of my family and his, I prayed that God would help me to believe, to live and to teach his Word, no matter the cost. I wanted to keep a completely open heart and mind to Sacred Scripture and the Holy Spirit and whatever sources would lead me to deeper insights into God's Word.

Meanwhile, I was also hired as a part-time instructor at a local Presbyterian seminary. The subject of my first class was the Gospel of John, on which I was also doing a sermon series at the church. In my studies, I was keeping a couple of chapters ahead of the series. When I got to the sixth chapter of the Gospel in my preparation, I spent weeks of careful study on the following verses (Jn 6:52–68):

> The Jews then disputed among themselves, saying, "How can this man give us his flesh to eat?" So Jesus said to them, "Truly, truly, I say to you, unless you eat the flesh of the Son of man and drink his blood, you have no life in you; he who eats my flesh and drinks my blood has eternal life, and I will raise him up at the last day. For my flesh is food indeed, and my blood is drink indeed. He who eats my flesh and drinks my blood abides in me, and I in him. As the living Father sent me, and I live because of the Father, so he who eats me will live because of me. This is the bread which came down from heaven, not such as the fathers ate and died; he who eats this bread will live for ever. . . ."
>
> After this many of his disciples drew back and no longer went about with him. Jesus said to the twelve, "Do you also wish to go away?" Simon Peter answered him, "Lord, to whom shall we go? You have the words of eternal life."

Immediately, I wondered about what my professors had taught me—and what I was preaching to my congregation—about the Eucharist being a mere symbol—a profound symbol, to be sure, but just a symbol.

But after lots of prayer and study, I realized that Jesus could not have been speaking figuratively when he taught us to eat his flesh and drink his blood. The Jews in his audience would not have been outraged and scandalized by a mere symbol. Besides, if they had misunderstood Jesus to be speaking literally—when he meant his words to be taken figuratively—he could have easily clarified his point. In fact, since many disciples stopped following Jesus because of this teaching (v. 60), he would have been morally obliged to explain the saying in purely symbolic terms.

But he never did. Nor did any Christian, for over one thousand years, ever deny the Real Presence of Christ in the Eucharist. No wonder. So I did what any pastor or seminary professor would do if he wanted to keep his job. I promptly stopped my sermon series on the Gospel of John at the end of chapter 5 and basically skipped over chapter 6 in my classroom lectures.

Although my parishioners and students were getting excited about the rest of my teaching, they were getting a sense that this was not historic, traditional Presbyterianism. I could not bring myself to tell them that what they were hearing—and responding so enthusiastically to—echoed ideas from Scripture that somehow, somewhere, the Catholic Church had discovered along the way.

One evening, after hours of study, I stopped in the living room and announced to Kimberly that I didn't think we were going to remain Presbyterians. I was so convinced from Scripture of the need to give higher priority to the sacraments and liturgy than the Presbyterian tradition gave them that I suggested we consider the Episcopal tradition.

She slumped down in the armchair and started crying. "Scott, my father's a Presbyterian minister. My uncle's a

Presbyterian minister. My brother's preparing to be a Presbyterian minister. And you are a Presbyterian minister. I don't want to stop being a Presbyterian."

She had made her point. But what she didn't know was that I was hoping at the time that the trail could end in the Episcopal church, though I wasn't sure.

The class I taught on the Gospel of John had gone so well that they asked me to teach some more classes the following semester. In fact, they asked me to go full-time next term, and those classes went even better.

In my Church history class, one of my better students (an ex-Catholic) made a presentation on the Council of Trent. Following the presentation, he posed a whopper-stopper question I'd never heard before.

He said, "Professor Hahn, you've shown us that *sola fide* isn't scriptural—how the battle cry of the Reformation is off-base when it comes to interpreting Paul. As you know, the other battle cry of the Reformation was *sola scriptura*: the Bible alone is our authority, rather than the Pope, Church councils or Tradition. Professor, where does the Bible teach that 'Scripture alone' is our sole authority?"

I looked at him and broke into a cold sweat.

I had never heard that question before. In seminary I had a reputation for being a sort of socratic gadfly, always asking the toughest questions, but this one had never occurred to me.

I said what any professor caught unprepared would say, "What a dumb question!" As soon as the words left my mouth, I stopped dead in my tracks, because I'd sworn that, as a teacher, I would never say those words.

But the student was not intimidated—he knew it wasn't a dumb question. He looked me right in the eyes and said, "Just give me a dumb answer."

I said, "First, we would go to Matthew 5:17. Then we would look at 2 Timothy 3:16–17, 'All Scripture is inspired by God and profitable for teaching, for reproof, for correction and for training in righteousness that the man of God may be complete, equipped for every good work.' And we'd look at what Jesus says about tradition in Matthew 15."

His response was penetrating. "But Professor, Jesus wasn't condemning all tradition in Matthew 15 but rather corrupt tradition. When 2 Timothy 3:16 says 'all Scripture', it doesn't say that 'only Scripture' is profitable. Prayer, evangelizing and many other things are also essential. And what about 2 Thessalonians 2:15?"

"Yeah, 2 Thessalonians 2;15", I said weakly. "What does that say again?"

"Paul tells the Thessalonians, 'So then, brethren, stand firm and hold to the traditions which you were taught by us, either by word of mouth or by letter.' "

I shot back, "You know, John, we're straying from the topic. Let's move on and I'll share something on this next week."

I could tell he wasn't satisfied. Neither was I. As I drove home on the beltway that night, I stared up at the stars and moaned, "Lord, what's happening? Where *does* Scripture teach *sola scriptura*?"

There were two pillars on which Protestants based their revolt against Rome—one had already fallen, the other was shaking. I was scared.

I studied all week long. I got nowhere. So I called some friends. I got no farther. Finally, I called two of the best theologians in America as well as some of my former professors.

Those I consulted were shocked that I would raise

such a question. They were even more dismayed that I wasn't satisfied with their answers.

To one professor I said, "Maybe I'm suffering from amnesia, but somehow I've forgotten the simple reasons why we believe the Bible is our sole authority."

"Scott, what a dumb question!"

"Just give me a dumb answer."

"Scott," he responded, "you really can't demonstrate *sola scriptura* from Scripture. The Bible doesn't expressly declare that it is the Christian's only authority. In other words, Scott, *sola scriptura* is essentially the historic confession of the Reformers, over and against the Catholic claim that it is Scripture *plus* the Church and Tradition. For us, then, it is a theological presupposition, our starting point rather than a proven conclusion."

Then he offered me the same Scripture texts I had given my student, and I gave him the same penetrating responses.

"What more is there?" I wanted to know.

"Scott, look at what the Catholic Church teaches! Obviously Catholic Tradition is wrong."

"Obviously, it's wrong", I agreed. "But where is the basic notion of tradition condemned? Further, what did Paul mean when he required the Thessalonians to hold fast to *tradition*, both written and oral?" I kept pushing. "Isn't this ironic? We insist that Christians can believe only what the Bible teaches. But the Bible doesn't teach that *it* is our *only* authority!"

I asked another theologian, "What for you is the pillar and foundation of truth?"

He said, "The Bible, of course!"

"Then why does the Bible say in 1 Timothy 3:15 that the Church is the pillar and foundation of truth?"

"You set me up, Scott!"

"I'm the one who feels set up!"

"But, Scott, which church?"

"How many applicants for the job are there? I mean, how many churches even claim to be the pillar and foundation of truth?"

"Does this mean you're becoming Roman Catholic, Scott?"

"I hope not."

I felt the ground shaking, as though somebody was pulling the carpet out from under my feet. This question was larger than all the others, and nobody had an answer.

Shortly thereafter, the chairman of the board at the seminary approached me, to invite me, on behalf of the trustees, to accept a full-time position as dean of the seminary. This offer was based on the fact that my courses had gone so well and the students were excited.

This was the job I dreamed of getting by the time I was fifty! And here it was being dropped in my lap at the ripe old age of twenty-six. Though I couldn't tell him why, I had to say no. When I went home that night, I had to tell my wife about the offer.

"Kimberly, there is nothing in the world I would rather do than teach at the seminary level. But I want to know I am teaching the truth. For someday I will stand before Christ and give an account for what I have taught his people. It won't be enough for me to hide behind my denomination and professors. I need to be able to look him right in the eyes and say, 'Lord, I taught them whatever you taught me in your Word.' And Kimberly, I am no longer sure what that is, and I can't teach until I am." Then I braced myself for her response.

She graciously replied, "That's what I respect so much

about you, Scott. But this means we'll have to trust the Lord to provide a job."

God bless her.

This conversation led to another painful decision. I announced my resignation to the elders of Trinity Presbyterian Church.

At this point, I didn't know what I was going to do, but I knew I had to have integrity. I could not teach as a pastor until I had more clarity. Kimberly and I cast ourselves on the Lord and prayed to know the next step.

All I knew was that I wanted to believe, understand, teach and love whatever God revealed in his Word.

Kimberly:

Our arrival in Virginia began what I would describe as "The Tale of Four Seasons". We entered into a *"summertime"* of our dreams coming true. Scott was the minister at Trinity Presbyterian Church, teacher at Fairfax Christian School and, later that year, an instructor at Dominion Theological Institute. I was the pastor's wife, which I had always hoped to be, and I was becoming a mother for the first time.

Scott preached and taught, pouring out his heart after many hours of study and preparation, and I was delighted to sit under his teaching. We also made many new friends and were close to seminary friends who had just relocated nearby, which greatly helped our adjustment to the move.

On December 4, 1982, Michael Scott was born. How he transformed our marriage! All of life had greater meaning because we wanted to share it with him. It was so exciting to have a little person to sing to, to pray with and to tell everything I could think of about the Lord. Residual selfishness, which Scott and I had not noticed in ourselves, challenged us day by day (and night by night), which in turn taught us more deeply about the Lord than ever before.

Scott began to study liturgy more and made interesting changes in our order of worship. We changed to weekly communion, which, for a Presbyterian church, is rather unusual. Though we received communion more often, we still believed it was only a symbolic representation of Christ's sacrifice and nothing more. However, Scott's study in the Gospel of John and Hebrews in preparation for classes and sermons was giving him new questions to ponder, which, at times, were unsettling to him.

Scott gained many insights from the early Church Fathers, some of which he shared in his sermons. This was rather unexpected for both of us, because we had hardly ever read the early Church Fathers when we were in seminary. In fact, in our senior year we had complained loudly to friends about possible creeping Romanism when a course was offered by an Anglican priest on the early Church Fathers. Yet here was Scott quoting them in sermons!

One night Scott came out of his study and said, "Kimberly, I have to be honest. You know some of the questions I'm wrestling with. I don't know how long we are going to be Presbyterians. We may become Episcopalians."

I sank into a chair in the living room and began to cry. I thought: If I'd wanted to be Episcopalian, I'd have married one! And I didn't want to be Episcopalian. How far was Scott going to go on this "pilgrimage"? I knew one thing for sure, he didn't even think thoughtful Catholics could be Christians, so there was no chance that could happen.

And then came that fateful night when a student (an ex-Catholic, to boot) asked, "Where does the Bible teach *sola scriptura?*"

As Scott groped for an answer to give this young man, he shared with me his primary concern that the split between Protestants and Catholics at the time of the Reformation was based on two major tenets: We are justified by faith alone, and our authority is Scripture alone. Scott and I had already studied the issue of justification and no longer subscribed to the Protestant conception. But what if the authority of Scripture alone was not scriptural? What would that mean?

At the end of the academic year, the board of the seminary asked Scott to be dean. Dean! At the age of twenty-six! Yet Scott turned down this wonderful offer. He said he was not sure he could continue to be a pastor right then either because he had so many important and unanswered questions. He needed a place where he could study these issues that were troubling him so much, so that he could teach with integrity, convinced from the Word of God that he was teaching truth.

Though this was difficult to hear, I appreciated his integrity. No question about it—he had to be able to face Christ on Judgment Day and answer why he had taught what he had taught. This decision drove us to our knees.

Through much prayer we decided to return to our college town, Grove City. It was after we had decided to go—and even rented a house there—that the president of the college called Scott and offered him a position. We took this as a sign of God's blessing on our decision to return to Grove City, and with that we packed our bags and left dear friends to begin a new phase of our family's life.

Scott, Kimberly and Michael (age three months). March, 1983.

5

Scott's Search for the Church

Scott:

We decided to return to the college town where we had
met. We wanted to plant our family in a nice, small town
where we knew many people, while I hoped to find a job
that would leave my evenings free to study the difficult
issues that were troubling me.

I accepted an offer to serve as assistant to the president
of Grove City College. It was an ideal job. I worked
nine-to-five in the administration, while serving as a part-
time guest instructor in the theology department, teaching one course each semester. It left me with my evenings free for study.

One of my former college professors asked why we
were moving back to town. He had heard that I had been
a pastor of a growing church in Virginia, along with
teaching at a local seminary. He was baffled by our move.
I suggested that life around the D.C. beltway was too
fast-paced. We wanted to raise a family. . . . I couldn't
tell him all the reasons why—because I still wasn't sure
myself.

Shortly after our move, on a visit to my in-laws in
Cincinnati, I found a used bookstore that had bought out
the library of a deceased priest who was also a well-
known Scripture scholar. Over the next two years, I
walked away with about thirty boxes of his theology

books. I began intensively devouring these for five, six, sometimes even seven hours at night. I was able to get through at least two hundred books. For the first time, I was hearing Catholicism from the horse's mouth, so to speak.

Sometimes, in the evening, I would play a game with Kimberly that I called "Name That Theologian". On one occasion, I read a section from Vatican II and asked her, "Who is the author?"

She said, "That sounds like one of your sermons back in Virginia. You don't know how much I miss hearing you preach!"

"That wasn't me. That was Vatican II. Can you believe it?"

"I don't want to hear that", was her only reply.

I continued reading all kinds of books about Catholic theology. One evening I stopped in the dining room en route to my study and said, "Kimberly, I have to be honest. I'm reading a lot of Catholic books these days, and I think God might be calling me into the Catholic Church."

To which Kimberly quickly replied, "Can't we become Episcopalians?" Apparently there was something more dreaded than becoming Episcopalian—anything but Catholic.

I went to a Byzantine Catholic seminary just to attend their vespers liturgy. It wasn't a Mass; it was just prayer, with all the prostrations, incense and icons, the smells and the bells. When it was over, a seminarian asked me, "What do you think?" I simply muttered, "Now I know why God gave me a body: to worship the Lord with his people in liturgy."

I drove back home, searching and asking God for help. I still hoped to find one fatal flaw that would keep me from "swimming the Tiber", as we say, or from "pope-ing".

So I started looking into Orthodoxy. I met with Peter Gilquist, an evangelical convert to Antiochene Ortho-doxy, to hear why he chose Orthodoxy over Rome. His reasons reinforced my sense that Protestantism was wrong; but I also thought that his defense of Orthodoxy over Catholicism was unsatisfying and superficial. Upon closer examination, I found the various Orthodox churches to be hopelessly divided among themselves, sim-ilar to the Protestants, except that the Orthodox were split along the lines of ethnic nationalisms; there were Orthodox bodies that called themselves Greek, Russian, Ruthenian, Rumanian, Bulgarian, Hungarian, Serbian and so on. They have coexisted for centuries, but more like a family of brothers who have lost their father.

Further study led me to conclude that Orthodoxy was wonderful for its liturgy and tradition but stagnant in the-ology. In addition, I became convinced that it was mis-taken in doctrine, having rejected certain teachings of Scripture and the Catholic Church, especially the *filioque* clause ("and the Son") that had been added to the Nicene Creed. In addition, their rejection of the Pope as head of the Church seemed to be based on imperial politics, more than on any serious theological grounds. This helped me to understand why, throughout their history, Orthodox Christians have tended to exalt the Emperor and the State over the Bishop and the Church (otherwise known as "Caesaropapism"). It occurred to me that Russia had been reaping the consequences of this Orthodox outlook throughout the twentieth century.

Ever since seminary, I frequently "talked shop" in late-night marathon phone conversations with my old friend from Gordon-Conwell, Gerry Matatics. He was a real kindred spirit who loved the Bible as much as I and hated the Catholic Church even more. At the time, he was pastoring a Presbyterian church in Harrisburg. Both of us shared the conviction that the Catholic Church was totally unlike certain Protestant denominations, such as the Methodists, the Lutherans or the Assembly of God— all of which we thought were a little off here and there, on this or that point of doctrine.

But if the Catholic Church was wrong, it was more than a little off, because no denomination on earth made the kinds of outrageous claims that Rome made for itself. For instance, the Methodists never claimed to be the one and only true Church founded by Jesus; nor did the Lutherans claim to have as their head a Pope who was Christ's infallible vicar on earth; nor was the Assembly of God run by leaders claiming an unbroken line of succession going all the way back to Peter.

Like Cardinal Newman before us, Gerry and I could see that if the Catholic Church was wrong, it was nothing less than diabolical. On the other hand, if it was right, it must have been divinely established and preserved; but that was hardly a serious option for either of us.

To be honest, I dreaded the moment when Gerry would find out what I was reading and thinking about. But since we talked so much and so long, I figured that it was only a matter of time.

One night it finally happened. We had been talking about Scripture for over an hour when, all of the sudden, I got the urge to read him a passage from *The Spirit and Forms of Protestantism*, by Father Louis Bouyer. I wasn't going to tell him the title, author or even his denominational affiliation. I just wanted to get his reaction.

After a long pause, he gasped, "Wow, that's good stuff, Scott. Who were you reading from?"

His response really threw me off. I hadn't planned on his liking it. What should I do now?

I replied rather weakly, "Louis Bouyer".

"Bouyer? Never heard of him. What is he? An Anglican?"

"No."

"That's okay, Scott. I'll read Lutherans."

"No, he's not Lutheran."

"Well, what is he? Methodist?"

"No."

"C'mon, Scott, what is this, twenty questions? Stop playing games. What is he?"

I covered my mouth and murmured, "Catholic."

I heard Gerry knock his phone and say, "Scott, I must have a bad connection—I couldn't make out what you said."

A little less softly, I muttered, "I said, he's a Catholic."

"Scott, there must *really* be something wrong with my phone. I could have sworn you just said he's a Catholic."

"I did, Gerry. In fact, I've been reading lots of Catholics lately."

All of a sudden it began gushing out. "I have to tell you, Gerry, I've struck gold. I don't know why, but we were never told at seminary about the most brilliant theological minds of modern times, men like Henri de Lubac, Reginald Garrigou-Lagrange, Joseph Ratzinger, Hans Urs von Balthasar, Josef Pieper, Jean Daniélou, Christopher Dawson and Matthias Scheeben. It's incredible— even if they're wrong—it's a gold mine!"

Gerry was stunned. "Whoa, Scott. Slow down! Wait a second. What's going on?"

I sighed, "Gerry, I need your help."

He said, "I'll help you. Brother, I'll help you. Give me a list of titles, and I'll give you a list of the best anti-Catholic books I know."

So I sent Gerry a list of the best books I had read on Catholic theology. When Gerry's list arrived, I found that I had already read every title he recommended.

A month later Gerry called back.

Kimberly could hardly contain her excitement. She had been hoping and praying that God would send help.

She whispered to me as I picked up the phone, "Finally, someone is going to take you seriously, Scott. I'll be praying for your conversation."

In that month since our previous phone call Gerry had read every single title on my list and then some. Now he even asked, "Could you give me some more titles? I really want to be fair."

For Kimberly, Gerry was a "knight in shining armor" sent by God to rescue her husband from heresy. And he had the credentials to do it. He was a Phi Beta Kappa scholar who had majored in classical Greek and Latin and studied Hebrew and Aramaic. He was more than ready for combat.

I said, "Sure, Gerry. I'll send you some more titles. Gladly."

About a month later, we talked for three or four hours, until around three in the morning. Afterward, I slipped quietly into bed so that I wouldn't wake Kimberly.

She whispered, "How did it go?" She was wide awake.

"It went great."

She sat up in bed. "Really? I knew the Lord would hear my prayers and Gerry would help."

"Gerry is helping. He has read through every book."

"Scott, he's really taking you seriously."

"Oh, he sure is."

She asked, "So, what does he think?"

"Well, so far he says there's not a single Catholic doctrine that he can't find scriptural support for."

These were not the words Kimberly had expected to hear.

"What?" she replied.

In the darkness I could feel her slump back into bed. She buried her face in the pillow and began to sob. I tried to comfort her, but she said, "Don't touch me. I feel so betrayed."

"I'm sorry. I'm sorry. Gerry's still working on it, so don't give up hope."

Gerry, who was supposed to rescue me, ended up getting swept off his feet. He began his own in-depth study of Scripture, and, as a result, he saw how much sense the Catholic Faith made in light of covenant theology and the early Church Fathers.

We talked long distance a number of times, trying to figure out together how the Catholic Church was wrong. It had to be—that was the given. How could we prove it? Whenever we felt we had found the Achilles heel, not only would we discover an answer, but an unanswerable answer. We were getting nervous.

Meanwhile Kimberly had just given birth to our second child, Gabriel. Another son meant greater joy than ever; at the same time it intensified the need for resolution. As a busy mother, with little free time to study theology, Kimberly grew anxious and confused. But I kept pressing on like a zealot.

It was hard because Kimberly really didn't want to talk about the Catholic Church. It was even harder because several priests I visited really didn't want to talk about the Church, either. I would sneak out to find a priest to answer some of my remaining questions. I was discouraged by one after another.

I asked one of them, "Father Jim, how would I go about converting to the Catholic Church?"

"First," he said, "please don't call me 'Father'. Second, I don't think you really need to convert. Ever since Vatican II, it's not ecumenical to convert! The best thing for you to do is simply to be the best Presbyterian you can be. You'll do more good for the Catholic Church if you just stay put."

Amazed, I responded, "Look, Father, I'm not asking you to twist my arm and force me to become a Catholic. I think God might be calling me into the Church, where I've found my home, my covenant family."

He replied icily, "Well, if you want someone to help you convert, you've come to the wrong person."

I was stunned.

On the way home, I prayed that the Lord would lead me to someone who would answer my questions. A thought came to me: perhaps I should enroll in theology courses at a Catholic university.

I applied to the doctoral program at Duquesne University in Pittsburgh. I was accepted and awarded a scholarship. Each week I drove down for classes. I was the only Protestant in some of my seminars and the only student defending Pope John Paul II! It was weird. I found myself explaining to priests (and even ex-priests) how certain Catholic beliefs were grounded in Scripture, especially in its theology of the covenant. It wasn't clear that I was going to find answers to my questions there.

Sometimes a Catholic friend from Grove City would

accompany me down to Pittsburgh, where he met with Father John Debicki, a priest of Opus Dei. I had never heard of Opus Dei before. All I knew was that this was a priest who took my questions seriously, gave thoughtful responses and let me know he was praying for me. He was such a humble man—I didn't discover until later that he had studied theology in Rome, where he received his doctorate.

Several Catholics at Duquesne came to me on the side and said, "You can really make Scripture sing. It sounds Catholic when you talk."

I said, "I think it is Catholic."

Later that night, I wondered aloud to Kimberly: "Why are Gerry and I the only ones to see these Catholic ideas in Scripture?"

Kimberly replied somewhat cynically, "Maybe the Church you're reading about doesn't exist any more."

I wondered if she might be right. It was frightening. I knew Kimberly was praying for help for me. I was praying a lot, too.

Someone mailed me a plastic Rosary. As I looked at those beads, I felt I was confronting the toughest obstacle of all: Mary. (Catholics have no idea how hard Marian doctrines and devotions are for Bible Christians.) So many doctrines of the Catholic Church had proven to be sound biblically that I decided to step out in faith on this one.

I locked myself in my office and quietly prayed. I said, "Lord, the Catholic Church has gotten it right ninety-nine times out of a hundred. The only major obstacle left is Mary. I apologize in advance if you're offended by what I'm about to do. . . . Mary, if you are even half of what the Catholic Church says, please take this specific petition—which seems impossible—to the Lord for me through this prayer."

I then prayed my first Rosary. I prayed it again for that intention several more times the next week, but then I forgot about it. Three months later, I realized that from the day I prayed my first Rosary, that seemingly impossible situation had been completely reversed. My petition had been granted!

I was struck by my inattention and ingratitude. I immediately thanked God for his mercy, took up the Rosary and have been praying it daily ever since. It is a most powerful prayer—an incredible weapon, one that highlights the scandal of the Incarnation: the Lord took a humble, peasant virgin and raised her up to be the one who would give sinless human nature to the second Person of the Trinity, so that he could become our Savior.

A short while later, I got a call from an old college friend. Apparently he had heard I was flirting with the "whore of Babylon", as he put it. He didn't waste any words.

"So, Scott, are you worshiping Mary yet?"

"C'mon, Chris, you know that Catholics don't *worship* Mary, they simply venerate her."

"Really, Scott, what's the difference? There's no biblical basis either way."

I didn't know what to say. Fingering my Rosary, I whispered to Mary for help. Emboldened, I replied, "You might be surprised."

"Oh, really, how so?"

I just started saying whatever came into my mind. "It's really quite simple, Chris. Just remember two basic biblical principles. First, you know that, as a man, Christ fulfilled God's law perfectly, including the commandment to honor his father and mother. The Hebrew word for honor, *kaboda^h*, literally means 'to glorify'. So Christ didn't just honor his heavenly Father; he also perfectly honored his earthly mother, Mary, by bestowing his own divine glory upon her.

"The second principle is even easier: the imitation of Christ. So, we simply imitate Christ not just by honoring our own mothers but also by honoring whomever he honors—and with the same honor that he bestows."

There was a long pause before Chris said, "I never heard it put that way before."

To be frank, I hadn't either. "Chris, that's just a summary of what the Popes have been saying for centuries about devotion to Mary."

He started back on the attack. "The Popes are one thing, but where is it in Scripture?"

I fired back instinctively, "Chris, Luke 1:48 says 'Henceforth all generations will call me blessed.' This is what the Rosary does, Chris, it fulfills that Scripture."

There was a long pause, before Chris quickly changed the subject.

From then on, I kept sensing how praying the Rosary actually deepened my own theological penetration of Scripture. The key was meditating upon the fifteen mysteries, of course, but I found the prayer itself imparted a certain theological outlook for pondering all the mysteries of our Faith according to something that went beyond (but not against) the rational powers of the intellect, what certain theologians have called the "logic of love".

This "logic of love" I first discovered by contemplating the Holy Family in Nazareth, the model for every household. This, in turn, pointed to the covenant and ultimately back to God's own inner life as the one eternal

Holy Family: the Father, the Son and the Holy Spirit. This beautiful and compelling vision started to fill my heart and mind; but I still wasn't sure that the Catholic Church should be identified as the earthly expression of God's covenant family. A lot more study and prayer were needed for that.

During this time, Gerry and I kept up our phone conversations. One day he called to invite me to join him in a get-together with one of our more brilliant mentors, Dr. John Gerstner, a Harvard-trained, Calvinist theologian with strong anti-Catholic convictions. Gerry told him that we were seriously considering the claims of the Catholic Church; so he was more than willing to meet with us to answer our questions.

Gerry made the arrangements. We could bring our Greek New Testaments, Hebrew Bibles, Latin council texts and whatever else we wanted; and we should be ready to debate anything, but especially *sola fide*.

All three of us were to meet for supper at the York Steak House not far from Gerry's home in Harrisburg. This meant Dr. Gerstner and I would drive together for several hours there and back. I was both excited and nervous to interact with such a devout and erudite scholar.

As Dr. Gerstner and I drove out, we had four hours of intensive theological discussion. I was sharing this backlog of arguments that I had been storing up, all about the Catholic Church being the climax of salvation history in the Old Testament and the embodiment of the New Covenant.

Dr. Gerstner listened carefully, responding to each point with concern and respect. He seemed to regard my arguments as somewhat novel; all the while he insisted they did not require anyone to join the Roman Catholic Church, which he referred to as "the synagogue of Satan".

At one point, he asked, "Scott, what biblical support do you find for the Pope?"

"Dr. Gerstner, you know how Matthew's Gospel emphasizes Jesus' role as the Son of David and the King of Israel, sent by his Father to inaugurate the Kingdom of heaven? I believe that Matthew 16:17–19 shows us how Jesus establishes it. He gave Simon three things: first, the new name of 'Peter' (or Rock); second, his pledge to build his Church upon Peter; and third, the keys of the Kingdom of heaven. It's that third item I find so interesting.

"When Jesus speaks of the 'keys of the Kingdom', he is referring to an important Old Testament passage, Isaiah 22:20–22, where Hezekiah, the royal heir to David's throne and King of Israel in Isaiah's day, replaced his old Prime Minister, Shebna, with a new one named Eliakim. Everyone could tell which one of the royal cabinet members was the new Prime Minister since he was given the 'keys of the kingdom'. By entrusting to Peter the 'keys of the Kingdom', Jesus established the office of Prime Minister for administering the Church as his Kingdom on earth. The 'keys' are a symbol, then, of Peter's office and primacy to be handed on to his successor; thus it has been handed down throughout the ages."

He responded, "That's a clever argument, Scott."

"So, how do we Protestants refute it?"

He said, "Well, I'm not sure I've heard it before. I'd have to think some more about it. Go on with your other points."

So I went on to describe how the covenant family was the overarching principle or master idea of the Catholic Faith. It explained Mary as our mother, the Pope as our father, the saints as our brothers and sisters, the feast days as anniversaries and birthdays.

"Dr. Gerstner, it all makes so much sense once you see the covenant at the center of Scripture."

He listened carefully. "Now Scott, I think you're taking this covenant thing too far."

"Maybe I am, Dr. Gerstner, but I'm absolutely convicted that the covenant is central to all of Scripture, just as the greatest Protestants like John Calvin and Jonathan Edwards have taught; but I'm also convinced that the covenant is not a contract, as they understood it, but rather a sacred family bond between God and his people. If I'm wrong on either point, show me where. Please. You could save my career."

He said, "Let's wait until we are with Gerry."

Once we arrived at the meeting place, we hacked away for hours and hours on many issues, but primarily justification. I was presenting the Catholic view that justification was not merely acquittal but was, in the view of the Council of Trent, divine sonship. For six hours Gerry and I argued various Catholic positions; none was refuted. We also raised many questions that were not answered to our satisfaction.

At the end, Gerry and I looked at each other—we were both pale. This was a shock for us. We had been hoping and praying that someone could save us from having to undergo the humiliation of converting.

When we were alone briefly, I said, "Gerry, I feel betrayed by our Reformed tradition. I came here thinking we were going to get blown out of the water. But the Catholic Church didn't lose on a single point. The texts quoted from the Council of Trent have been taken out of context. Inadvertently, he's been misrepresenting the canons by isolating them from the definitions stated in the decrees."

On the way home I talked a lot more with Dr. Gerstner. I asked him to show me where the Bible taught *sola scriptura*. I did not hear a single new argument. Instead he posed a question to me. "Scott, if you agree that we now possess the inspired and inerrant Word of God in Scripture, then what more do we need?"

I replied, "Dr. Gerstner, I don't think that the primary issue concerns what we need; but since you ask the question, I'll give you my impression. Ever since the Reformation, over twenty-five thousand different Protestant denominations have come into existence, and experts say there are presently five new ones being formed every week. Every single one of them claims to be following the Holy Spirit and the plain meaning of Scripture. God knows we must need something more.

"I mean, Dr. Gerstner, when our nation's founders gave us the Constitution, they didn't leave it at that. Can you imagine what we'd have today if all they had given us was a document, as good as it is, along with a charge like 'May the spirit of Washington guide each and every citizen'? We'd have anarchy—which is basically what we Protestants *do* have when it comes to church unity. Instead, our founding fathers gave us something besides the Constitution; they gave us a government—made up of a President, Congress and a Supreme Court—all of which are needed to administer and interpret the Constitution. And if that's just enough to govern a country like ours, what would it take to govern a worldwide Church?

"That's why, personally, Dr. Gerstner, I'm beginning to think that Christ didn't leave us with just a book and his Spirit. In fact, he never mentions a thing about writing to his apostles anywhere in the Gospels; besides, fewer than half of them even wrote books that were included in the New Testament. What Christ *did* say—to Peter—was, 'Upon this rock, I will build my Church . . . , and the gates of hades will not prevail against it.' So it makes more sense to me that Jesus left us with his Church—made up of a Pope, bishops and councils—all of which are needed to administer and interpret Scripture."

Dr. Gerstner gave a thoughtful pause. "That's all very interesting, Scott, but you said that you didn't think it was the primary issue? What, then, is the primary issue for you?"

"Dr. Gerstner, I think the primary issue is what the Scripture teaches about the Word of God, for nowhere does it reduce God's Word down to Scripture alone. Instead, the Bible tells us in many places that God's authoritative Word is to be found in the Church: her Tradition (2 Th 2:15; 3:6) as well as her preaching and teaching (1 Pet 1:25; 2 Pet 1:20–21; Mt 18:17). That's why I think the Bible supports the Catholic principle of *sola verbum Dei*, 'the Word of God alone', rather than the Protestant slogan, *sola scriptura*, 'Scripture alone'."

Dr. Gerstner responded by asserting—over and over again—that Catholic Tradition, the Popes and ecumenical councils all taught contrary to Scripture.

"Contrary to whose interpretation of Scripture?" I asked. "Besides, Church historians all agree that we got the New Testament from the Council of Hippo in 393 and the Council of Carthage in 397, both of which sent off their judgments to Rome for the Pope's approval. From 30 to 393 is a long time to be without a New Testament, isn't it? Besides, there were many other books that people back then thought might be inspired, such as the Epistle of Barnabas, the Shepherd of Hermas and the Acts of Paul. There were also several New Testament books, such as Second Peter, Jude and Revelation, that some thought should be excluded. So whose decision was trustworthy and final, if the Church doesn't teach with infallible authority?"

Dr. Gerstner calmly replied, "Popes, bishops and councils can and do make mistakes. Scott, how is it you can think that God renders Peter infallible?"

I paused for a moment. "Well, Dr. Gerstner, Protestants and Catholics agree that God most certainly rendered Peter infallible on at least a couple of occasions, when he wrote First and Second Peter, for instance. So if God could render him infallible when teaching authoritatively in print, then why couldn't he prevent him from errors when teaching authoritatively in person? Likewise, if God could do it with Peter—and the other apostles who wrote Scripture—then why couldn't he do it with their successors as well, especially since he could foresee the anarchy that would come if he didn't? Besides, Dr. Gerstner, how can we be sure about the twenty-seven books of the New Testament themselves being the infallible Word of God, since fallible Church councils and Popes are the ones who made up the list?"

I will never forget his response.

"Scott, that simply means that all we can have is a fallible collection of infallible documents!"

I asked, "Is that really the best that historic Protestant Christianity can do?"

"Yes, Scott, all we can do is make probable judgments from historical evidence. We have no infallible authority but Scripture."

"But, Dr. Gerstner, how can I be certain that it's really God's infallible Word that I am reading when I open up Matthew, or Romans, or Galatians?"

"Like I said, Scott, all we have is a fallible collection of infallible documents."

Once again, I felt very unsatisfied with his answers, though I knew he was representing the Protestant position faithfully. I sat there pondering what he had said about this, the ultimate issue of authority, and the logical inconsistency of the Protestant position.

All I said in response was, "Then it occurs to me, Dr. Gerstner, that when it comes right down to it, it must be the Bible *and* the Church—both or neither!"

I got home early the next morning. When I shared with Kimberly the results of our day together, she panicked. She had hoped that the previous day's conversation would end it all.

She exacted a pledge from me. "Please don't do this abruptly. It would be too painful."

I assured her, "If I convert, Kimberly, it won't be until 1990 at the earliest, I promise. And I will convert only if it is absolutely necessary; if these conclusions become inescapable." The year was 1985. That seemed like enough time to make an intellectually respectable move if I was going to convert.

She said, "Okay. I can live with that."

After much prayer we saw that it was necessary for me to work on this full time. We decided the best place to go would be Marquette University, where I had discovered there was a team of outstanding Catholic theologians who loved the Church and taught the Church's doctrine very well. In fact, there was a Jesuit professor of theology, Father Donald Keefe, who specialized in covenant theology. When we heard that Marquette had accepted me into the doctoral program in theology—and was offering me a full scholarship with a teaching assistantship—we felt the Lord's leading.

Little did I know, little did we know, that our marriage was about to embark upon a time darker and stormier than we could ever anticipate.

Kimberly:

When we returned to Grove City, we were moving into our season of "*fall*". The winds of change were beginning to blow. The colors were beautiful, but the changes they signaled were signs of dormition and death.

There was a change of pace as we resettled our family. Scott began his nine-to-five job as assistant to the president of Grove City College. I focused on Michael and renewing friendships.

Scott's job enabled him to have evenings free to study for hours every night. He went into his study and closed the door, and I did not want him to open it. I was not interested in knowing what he was reading. As long as he kept that door shut, it was just fine with me.

We were really beginning to grow apart in our convictions: in part I was busy, pregnant with our second child, and in part I was not interested. I was sure that he was going way out on a limb and that he was going to come back. The most important thing for me to do was to keep steady.

One night he interrupted my sleep with an enthusiastic thought, "Kimberly, do you realize that we are surrounded right here and now by Mary, the saints and countless angels?"

Quickly, I replied, "Not in my bedroom! No way!"

What Scott had said had startled me. Mary? He was thinking a lot more about her these days. It seemed that Catholics focused on Mary the way we focused on Jesus: she was the approachable one—you could hide in her skirts rather than face the Father in his anger; Mary was the broad back door into God's favor, while Jesus remained the narrow front door. Those thoughts were repugnant to me.

I once read about a man in Rome who was repairing the ceiling of a beautiful chapel one day when he observed an American woman enter the church and begin to pray. He thought he'd have a little fun, so he called down quietly, "This is Jesus." But the woman did not respond.

So he called out a little louder, "This is Jesus." Still no response.

Finally, the man called loudly, "This is Jesus!"

The woman looked up and yelled, "Be quiet, I'm talking to your mother!"

My exposure to how Catholics viewed Mary led me to think they were substituting love, devotion and even worship of Mary for love, devotion and worship of Jesus. I voiced these concerns to Scott. And he challenged me with the almost total neglect of Protestants even to talk about her, though at the very least she was the chosen, most highly favored woman of all time, who bore the Son of God and gave him his human nature. Protestants probably thought they were compensating for the overwhelming attention she was given by Catholics.

When I was approached to speak to the women's Christmas dinner at church, Scott challenged me to speak on Mary. So I gave a Bible study on Mary as a woman of God, not at all sharing any Catholic notions about her (which I didn't believe myself at that time). I cautioned the women not to fear honoring her as the Mother of our Lord because Jesus was both the Son of God and the Son of Mary.

Immediately following my talk, the two pastors' wives sang "What Child Is This", deliberately changing the last words of the chorus to "the babe, the Son of God" because one minister had voiced concern just before the dinner that the line "the babe, the Son of Mary" gave too much honor to Mary. What a case in point to illustrate my talk!

I was reminded of the lecture in seminary where Dr. Nicole had said that an ecumenical council had declared Mary to be *Theotokos*, Mother of God. At first we were all offended—she didn't create God! But he quickly clarified the purpose of that affirmation—it was necessary for our salvation for Jesus to be fully human as well as fully divine—two natures in the one Person of God the Son. Therefore, since Mary was the source of his human nature, she was the mother of Jesus; and since Jesus is God, she is the mother of God. There was no need to be offended by this truth, Dr. Nicole had pointed out, because it safeguarded our salvation.

One day, Scott paused in the dining room to say, "I'm reading a lot of Catholic books these days. God may be calling me into the Catholic Church."

"Can't we be Episcopalians?" was my immediate response. In the grand scheme of things, I preferred to remain Protestant as an Episcopalian than to become a

Roman Catholic. He smiled as if to say he understood why I asked. Then he asked me to pray for him.

I was happy to pray for him, but I didn't want to talk to him about his growing convictions. At this point I wanted to shelve Scott and put his growing convictions away, out of my reach. He gently tried to share some of his questions and conclusions with me when we were on a walk.

I said, "Scott, you are so bright. You could convince anyone of anything."

To which he replied, "So I have nothing to say to anyone?"

That cut me to the quick. How could I let myself say, or even think, that he had nothing to say to me about his theological reflections on issues when our whole marriage was based on precisely this kind of sharing?

I wasn't exempt from wrestling with the truth just because Scott was a persuasive person. But I didn't want to hear it. It was too scary—I had too much to lose. I should have been at least curious to know why he thought Catholicism was so biblical, of all things, because Scripture was the basis of my convictions. But I was too threatened by it to want to ask.

I began to feel as if I were married to a man I didn't marry. I had married a reformed Presbyterian, not just a generic Christian. However, Scott reminded me that what drew me to him was that he was a Bible-believing Christian, which he still was. He begged me to come alongside him in his study, but I couldn't. I didn't want to.

Scott, after all, had been anti-Catholic—he had thought one could not be a thoughtful Christian and remain Roman Catholic. I, on the other hand, had had a more balanced approach—Catholics can be Christians, but there was no need and certainly no desire on my part to want to be Catholic. Perhaps all his study would help him be less judgmental toward Catholics and more like me. But no longer condemning them did not mean joining them!

Scott felt that he was searching for "Mother Church" and that perhaps he had found her in Catholicism. In contrast, I was never keenly aware of a need to search (perhaps because I was raised in such a strong, evangelical family and church where that need had been met).

What Scott now believed compared to what he had believed when we were students in college seemed markedly different. Scott saw continuity where I saw only discontinuity. He explained it using an analogy: an acorn doesn't look like an oak tree, but it holds within itself the possibility of becoming an oak tree.

"The convictions I held in college and seminary are coming to a richer flowering than ever before. There is organic growth, even though my beliefs look different from what they were in the beginning. I still believe the Bible. I'm still a committed Christian", he would say.

The analogy was plausible, I had to admit. But it was also possible he was outsmarting himself and getting into real trouble theologically.

We sought some advice from my father, who urged me to stay connected with Scott's studies. Even though I didn't want to study, it would not help for us to grow at different paces.

I finally agreed to read one book, *The Faith of Our Fathers*, by Cardinal Gibbons. His book was simple, yet it was making too much sense. It angered me. Catholicism could not be that clear! I got so frustrated I threw the

book across the room, something I had never done before.

No, I thought, I was just going to hang on and hope
that Scott would make his way back to truth on his own.
I had my Master's in theology! Was I supposed to relearn
everything, go back to the ABCs of theology? I was too
busy with life to be able to do that.

The psalmist captures my thoughts at the time (Ps
69:13, 14, 16):

> But as for me, my prayer is to thee, O Lord. At an accept-
> able time, O God, in the abundance of thy steadfast love,
> answer me. With thy faithful help, rescue me from sink-
> ing in the mire. Answer me, O Lord, for thy steadfast love
> is good; according to thy abundant mercy, turn to me.

In the midst of the theological turmoil in our home, the
Lord blessed us with a dear son, Gabriel Kirk, on our fifth
wedding anniversary, August 18, 1984. When I delivered
him, I remembered a prayer Scott and I had prayed in the
middle of our first date—that God would raise up many
godly men. And I thought: Lord, is Gabriel, and, for that
matter, Michael, in part an answer to our prayers years
ago? It sure is the slow way to make disciples, but please
help us to raise them to be godly men for you.

Gabriel's first year of life was a busy time. Besides car-
ing for our two little sons, many good activities consumed time which otherwise might have been study time
to resolve the issues between Scott and me. I led three
Bible studies, chaired the community pro-life group and
helped found Life Advocates on the Grove City College
campus. Scott shifted from full-time college work to part-
time work with youth at two churches and the college.
He also began work on his doctorate at Duquesne Uni-

versity. Though it was a Catholic institution, he usually found himself being the lone defender of the Catholic Faith in class.

In the midst of the busy-ness, Scott was still studying. As I realized that the Catholic Church was not diminishing in Scott's interest, I began to feel the weight of what we would lose should Scott become Catholic. All kinds of dreams that previously we had shared would have to die—being a pastor-and-wife team, Scott returning to teach at Grove City College or Gordon-Conwell Theological Seminary and both of us traveling a circuit to speak on the reformed Protestant faith.

One night Scott told me he had begun praying the Rosary. I couldn't believe my ears! I didn't even know he owned one. This study and now practice of Catholicism were getting serious.

A friend of ours from seminary, Gerry Matatics, challenged Scott's theological direction. To Scott, I referred to him as my "knight in shining armor" who was going to save me from this fate. Gerry pursued Scott for lists of Catholic books. I was so grateful for that, especially because Gerry was so much like Scott—a person of conviction who really wanted the truth, no matter what.

But I'll never forget the night Scott came back to the bedroom after talking to Gerry for several hours and told me how excited Gerry was about the Catholic books he was reading!

All I could do was weep. My "knight in shining armor" was getting tarnished! If Gerry could not stop Scott, I couldn't imagine who could.

When Gerry arranged a meeting with Dr. Gerstner, I found my hopes soaring, only to have them dashed upon hearing Scott's report of the meeting.

Since the beginning of our relationship, Scott and I had grown and changed together, at least in minor ways, in our convictions. But by Scott's continuing to change and my refusing to change, we were both starting not to trust one another. The foundation of trust in our marriage was being shaken tremendously.

After one particularly agonizing day, I said to Scott, "I would never consider suicide, but I have begged God today to give me an illness that would kill me so that I can die and have all the questions laid to rest. Then you could find a nice little Catholic girl and get on with life."

Scott was devastated to hear me express such anguish. "Don't ever say or even think that again! I don't want some nice little Catholic girl. I want you."

This was the beginning of the "*winter*" of my soul. I remember where I stood in our living room when I felt the joy of the Lord depart. Except for a few brief times, it did not return for almost five years—a lack I had never before experienced in my life. The joy of the Lord that had been my strength and had encouraged my spirit had been blocked by my refusal to be open to study or to read or even to talk. I felt as though I were facing a wall that I did not know how to get over and was not sure I even had the will to try.

"Lord, the joy is gone. Who are you? I've known you all my life. I thought I understood you, but now I don't understand anything. Are you the God of the Catholics or the Protestants? I'm so confused." There did not seem to be an answer.

6

One Comes Home to Rome

Scott:

It was a mutual but difficult decision to move to Milwaukee to begin full-time doctoral study in theology and Sacred Scripture. I discovered that fall semester, in seminar after seminar, how true and beautiful Catholic doctrines could be and how compelling and practical the moral teachings of the Church were with regard to marriage, family and society. I heard myself speak up for the Catholic Faith even when Catholics wouldn't.

There were several Catholic students who *did* speak up for their Faith, and at the same time they were living and enjoying it. I shared an office with one of them, John Grabowski, who took me to his parish and introduced me to the eucharistic liturgy. Through John, I also became acquainted with an exceptional Catholic institution called Franciscan University of Steubenville, where he had studied theology as an undergraduate. He told me all about their emphasis on "dynamic orthodoxy". (Little did I know I would find myself teaching there five years later.)

Another doctoral student, Monica Migliorino Miller, inspired me in a couple of ways. First, she would hear me in class sounding like a Catholic; later on she would gently but firmly challenge me to follow through on my Catholic convictions. Second, through her courageous commitment to pro-life rescue work, Monica motivated Kimberly and me to get involved ourselves. As a result, Kimberly and I found much-needed common ground as pro-family activists in fighting abortion and pornography throughout the Milwaukee area.

I wrote papers defending and arguing orthodox Catholic positions. I wrote up my arguments on Matthew 16:17–19 in a thirty-page paper entitled "Peter and the Keys" for a course on the Gospel of Matthew. The professor, who was Protestant, cross-examined me for over an hour but said he found no fault with the argument.

Some of my non-Catholic friends felt that it was a glorious vision God was giving me, though they had no idea where it was leading me. It was capturing my imagination as well as my intellect.

I wrote another paper, one hundred pages long, entitled "*Familia Dei*: Towards a Theology of Covenant, Family and Trinity", in which I synthesized the results of more than ten years of research on the covenant. It was making more and more sense; if covenant means a family in which members share flesh and blood, then Christ instituted the Eucharist to enable us to share the flesh-and-blood bond of his New Covenant family, the Catholic Church.

Father John Debicki, my priest-friend in Pittsburgh, put me in touch with Layton Study Center, an Opus Dei center in Milwaukee. The friends I made there—both the priests and members—introduced me to a practical approach to prayer, work, family and apostolate that drew all the strengths from my evangelical experience into a solid Catholic plan of life. There I was taught and encouraged, as a layman, to find ways to turn my work into prayer. One of the married members, Chris Wolfe, was constantly challenging me to place the highest priority on my interior life.

Finally, the conversion process was becoming, super-naturally, a *romance* tale. The Holy Spirit was revealing that the Catholic Church, which used to horrify me so much, was really my home and my family. There was an exhilarating sense of homecoming as I discovered my father, mother, my older brothers and sisters.

Then one day, I made a "fatal blunder"—I decided that it was time for me to go to Mass on my own. Finally I resolved to darken the doors of Gesu, Marquette University's parish. Right before noon, I slipped quietly into the basement chapel for daily Mass. I wasn't sure what to expect; maybe I'd be alone with a priest and a couple of old nuns. I took a seat as an observer in the back pew.

All of a sudden lots of ordinary people began coming in off the streets—rank-and-file type folks. They came in, genuflected, knelt and prayed. Their simple but sincere devotion was impressive.

Then a bell rang and a priest walked out toward the altar. I remained seated; I still wasn't sure if it was safe to kneel. As an evangelical Calvinist, I had been taught that the Catholic Mass was the greatest sacrilege that a man could commit—to resacrifice Christ—so I wasn't sure what to do.

I watched and listened as the readings, prayers and responses—so steeped in Scripture—made the Bible come alive. I almost wanted to stop the Mass and say, "Wait. That line is from Isaiah; the song is from the Psalms. Whoa, you've got another prophet in that prayer." I found numerous elements from the ancient Jewish liturgy that I had studied so intensely.

All of a sudden I realized, this is where the Bible

belongs. This was the setting in which this precious family heirloom was meant to be read, proclaimed and expounded. Then we moved into the Liturgy of the Eucharist, where all my covenant conclusions converged.

I wanted to stop everything and shout, "Hey, can I explain what's happening from Scripture? This is great!" Instead I just sat there, famished with a supernatural hunger for the Bread of Life.

After pronouncing the words of consecration, the priest held up the Host. I felt as if the last drop of doubt had drained from me. With all of my heart, I whispered, "My Lord and my God. That's really you! And if that's you, then I want full communion with you. I don't want to hold anything back."

Then I remembered my promise: 1990. Oh, yes. I've got to regain control—I'm a Presbyterian, right? right! And with that, I left the chapel, not telling a soul where I had been or what I had done. But the next day I was back, and the next, and the next. Within a week or two I was hooked. I don't know how to say it, but I had fallen head over heels in love with our Lord in the Eucharist! His presence to me in the Blessed Sacrament was powerful and personal. As I sat in the back I began to kneel and pray with the others whom I now knew to be my brothers and sisters. I wasn't an orphan! I had found my family—it was God's family. Suddenly, 1990 seemed very far away.

Day after day, witnessing the entire drama of the Mass, I saw the covenant renewed right before my eyes. I knew Christ wanted me to receive him in faith, not just spiritually in my heart, but physically as well: onto my tongue, down my throat and into my whole body and soul. This was what the Incarnation was all about. This was the gospel in its fullness.

Each day after Mass, I spent a half hour to an hour praying the Rosary. I felt the Lord unleash his power through his Mother before the Blessed Sacrament. I begged him to open up my heart to show me his will.

"Lord, is this your supernatural call, or am I just caught up in some intellectual escapade?"

Things were beginning to speed up. Gerry called two weeks before Easter 1986 to announce that he and his wife, Leslie, were going to join the Church at the Easter Vigil.

I was stunned. "Gerry, I can't believe it. You were supposed to stop me from becoming a Catholic. You can't beat me to the Eucharist!" It hardly seemed fair.

"Scott, I'm not going to pry into your reasons for waiting, but God has already shown us enough to convince us to become Catholics this year."

So I went to the Lord in prayer. "Lord, what do you want *me* to do?" I remember praying that and thinking, I wonder why I haven't asked you that before now? "Lord, what *do* you want me to do?"

I was utterly taken aback when, to my surprise, I felt his response back to me, "What is it, my son, that *you* want to do?"

That was easy. I didn't have to think twice. "Father, I want to come home. I want to receive you, Jesus, my eldest Brother and Lord, in the Holy Eucharist."

It was as if the Lord quietly replied, "I'm not stopping you."

I felt exhilarated. It's impossible to describe. Then I realized that I had better check with the one person who *was* still trying to stop me. So I went downstairs to find Kimberly.

I said, "Kimberly, you'll never guess what Gerry just

told me. He said that he and Leslie are going to join the Catholic Church at Easter—in just two weeks."

Kimberly answered warily, "So what difference does that make?" She could see right through me.

"Well, I was just praying and asking the Lord for guidance. . . ."

"You said 1990, remember? You promised. Don't spiritualize your promise away."

I reluctantly acknowledged her point. "Yeah, I remember, 1990. But ever since I started going to daily Mass, I've felt Christ calling me to himself in the Holy Eucharist."

She listened quietly, deep hurt written all over her face.

"Kimberly, I don't know how to say this, but I'm afraid that I've reached the point where to delay obedience would be disobedience. Would you please pray about releasing me from this promise?"

At that point we felt pain that words cannot describe. After a time of prayer in another room, she came out and hugged me and said, "I'll release you from your promise, but I want you to know that I've never felt so deeply betrayed—so abandoned—in all my life."

It was hard for both of us.

Later that night I earnestly prayed, "Lord, why would you reveal your family to me and take me away from mine? Why have you shown me your Bride, the Church, and wrenched me apart from my own?"

During that time of prayer, the Lord seemed to say, "I am not calling you *in spite* of your love for Kimberly and the kids, but precisely *because* of your love—and my love—for them. Scott, you need the fullness of grace in the Eucharist in order for me to love them through you."

"Lord, why can't you tell her that yourself?" I asked.

I went to visit Monsignor Bruskewitz, who was then pastor at Saint Bernard's Church. (He has since become Bishop of Lincoln, Nebraska.) Saint Bernard's was the most orthodox and vital parish in the area. So I hoped that it would become a spiritual home for me. I was not disappointed.

Monsignor listened to my long theological odyssey. Being a trained theologian himself, he could appreciate the study and the struggle. He let me know that there would be no obstacle to my joining at the Easter Vigil. However, he was an astute pastor as well, so he recognized my need for some practical counsel.

He listened patiently to my plans for preparing myself for First Communion: a week of prayer to end with a three-day fast leading up to the Easter Vigil. He asked with gentle wisdom, "And where do Kimberly and the kids fit into all of this?"

I was embarrassed to admit that somehow they had been left out of my plan. Monsignor responded, "Scott, can I give you an alternate plan?"

"Sure", I replied contritely.

"Why not lavish your love and attention on them all week long, ending it with a wonderful family picnic at the park on Saturday afternoon, right before I give you First Communion that evening?" Thank God for pastoral wisdom.

Easter Vigil 1986 was a time of real supernatural joy but great natural sadness as well. I received the sacramental "grand slam": conditional baptism, reconciliation, confirmation and First Communion. I returned to my pew and sat down beside my grieving wife, whom I loved with all my heart. I put my arm around her, and we began to pray. I sensed how Christ himself, through the Eucharist within me, was reaching out to embrace us both.

It was as though the Lord was saying, "Scott, it isn't up to your feelings. Because of my gift to you in the Holy Eucharist, you can trust me now more than ever. I am now abiding in you, both body and soul, in a greater way than ever before."

I thank God for how he used Holy Communion to assure me that he would see us through the difficult times that lay ahead.

Kimberly:

Our move to Milwaukee was a move away from friends, family and church to a foreign place for both of us. We did not know anyone there before we arrived.

Though we went to a Protestant church together, I had the time that Scott didn't have to develop friendships there. His involvement in a Catholic university gave him more opportunities to meet Catholic friends there. So we continued to grow apart from each other in some ways, developing a number of separate friendships.

Most of my time was involved with the care of our two little sons. As we became more aware of the magnitude of the abortion and pornography industries around us—nine abortion clinics and five "adult" bookstores in downtown Milwaukee alone—I became very involved in activism. Consequently, I had very little time and less desire than time to study. I hoped that someone at Marquette would do what no one else so far had been able to do—stop Scott's defection to Rome.

I never suspected that Scott would move the date of being received into the Catholic Church from 1990 up to 1986. It was only ten days before Easter when he came from his study and said, "Kimberly, Gerry and Leslie are joining the Church this Easter Vigil. I need you to hear my heart: Ever since I began going to Mass at the University, I have ached, ached to receive the Lord in the Eucharist. And I am now so convicted of the truth of the Catholic Church that if I do not join the Church and receive the Lord in this way, I believe I'll be disobeying the Lord. We both know that delayed obedience is disobedience."

I was devastated! He had promised: "no sooner than 1990"! Yet I could see his deep conflict, between his promise on the one hand and his deepening conviction on the other. I could not stand in the way of his obedience to the Lord, no matter what questions it raised for his career or for our family's well-being. Scott needed to grant me the space necessary for the Holy Spirit to open my heart, and I needed to release him from the promise of waiting until I was ready to join him so that he could move ahead in obedience to the Lord as he understood it.

That night I wrote in my prayer journal about the intense loneliness and sense of betrayal I was feeling. I wrote, "Lord, to whom can I go about my deep hurt?" Somewhat sarcastically, I added, "And don't tell me Mary and the saints!!"

Easter was just ten days away. That meant we had only ten days to call family and let them know what we had basically kept quiet. We had just ten days to call theologian friends in the hopes they could unconvince him before he took the plunge into the Church. (The profes-

sors were put in a very difficult position—they were trying to answer objections Scott had spent years studying.
But the fact that so few tried to stop him, when he could
be plunging his soul into ruin and, later, with his gifts,
plunging other souls into ruin, increased the sense of
abandonment I felt.)

It was so difficult to know how to share in a way that
did not challenge the loyalty we both needed. If I had
shared with my family or Scott's how deep the pain was,
it could have caused a tremendous rift between them and
Scott. It was a loyalty issue for each of us. We had, for
the sake of our marriage and our family, to protect each
other and not share with other people the tremendous
pain that we were carrying. Yet that intensified the loneliness we both felt.

I had a very deep sense of betrayal. I had nothing
against Catholics, but I would not have dated one. Now I
was going to be married to one!

I went with Scott and one of my dear Protestant
friends to the Easter Vigil Mass. Chris Wolfe was there as
Scott's sponsor. At one point, Scott leaned over and told
me that Greg Wolfe (no relation) was going to be Gerry's
sponsor that same night when he and Leslie were
received into the Catholic Church out in Philadelphia. I
gave a wry smile but didn't say anything; it seemed more
than a little ironic that both men were being led by
Wolfes into the Catholic Church.

On the one hand, much of the service fascinated me—
there were numerous Scripture readings that followed
God's covenant-making throughout the Old Testament
leading up to Christ. (I had no idea that Catholics ever
read that much Scripture!) Many of the elements of the
service reminded me of Old Testament Jewish worship,

such as incense, bowing, an altar and a sacrifice. And the joy of the people was abundant (as if they really believed all they were doing and saying).

Yet, on the other hand, I was dying inside. Before my very eyes, Scott was vowing himself to a Church that would separate us for a while and perhaps even permanently. Never again would we take communion side by side unless one of us had a change of mind (and I could guess who that would have to be!). This great sign of Christian unity became our symbol of disunity. And the rejoicing of the people was like a dagger in my heart, for their joy was my unspeakable sorrow.

After Mass someone grabbed a camera and asked for a picture of everyone with Scott. I tried to step out of the group, but Scott insisted I be in the picture, too. I thought, why do I want to memorialize the worst night of my life? Though all of Scott's friends were very kind to me at the party afterward, it was excruciating to see the delight of all for him when our marriage was in the midst of the greatest challenge we had ever had.

Easter Vigil, 1986. Milwaukee, Wisconsin. Scott was received into the Church. Seen with concelebrants Fr. (now Bishop) Bruskewitz, Fr. Richard Roach and Fr. Donald Keefe.

7

The Struggles of a Mixed Marriage

Scott:

Curious friends began calling. The typical conversation would go something like this:

"Scott, I've just heard a vicious rumor—I know it can't be true—that you've become a Roman Catholic!"

I would say, "Yeah, can you believe it!? By the grace of God, I have become a Catholic, and I can't begin to thank him enough."

At which point, the conversation would usually end rather abruptly: "Oh, I see. Well, Scott, be sure to tell Kimberly I send along my prayers and greetings."

I suspect what they really meant to pass along were their condolences. For all practical purposes, I might as well have died and been replaced by a papist imposter, since that's the way most of them treated me.

Close friends became distant. Family members grew silent and turned away. One of my fellow graduate students—a devout evangelical—became a former friend overnight.

The irony was that, not so long ago, I had been far more anti-Catholic than any of them. In fact, most of them did not regard themselves as being anti-Catholic in any way, though they would not have raised an eyebrow if I had simply joined up with the Lutherans or Methodists. Instead I was made to feel like a leper.

There was never any desire for dialogue, much less debate. My reasons didn't matter, for I had done the unthinkable. I had committed a foul and traitorous misdeed.

But the pain and desolation could not compare with the joy and strength that came from knowing that I was doing God's will and obeying his Word. Compared with the privilege of going to daily Mass and receiving Holy Communion, my sacrifices seemed small. I also learned that such suffering can be united to Christ's eucharistic sacrifice with real effect and much consolation. Through it all, I was drawn into deeper intimacy with our Lord and our Lady. The pain made the romance more real.

Meanwhile Kimberly and I were sailing through even rougher waters. Days and weeks would pass without us sharing anything spiritual together. She was anything but eager to hear from me about the benefits of daily Mass and meditating on the mysteries of the Rosary. As my spiritual life surged forward, my marriage tumbled backward. What made it especially painful was our having shared such rich times of ministering together in the recent past. I found myself wondering, Will it ever be the way it was? Will our marriage even survive this period of trial and agony?

It was only the Lord working through the grace of the sacrament of matrimony that kept us going, as we both would attest. I once heard a priest say, "Marriage is not hard; it's just humanly impossible. That's why Christ reestablished it as a sacrament."

Kimberly kept hoping that someone would come along who would try to take me on. One Calvinist pastor named Wayne decided to meet with us. After a couple of four-hour sessions, Wayne told Kimberly, "The Pope will soon excommunicate Scott for being too scriptural."

"Where are his weak points?"

"Well, I don't know. His arguments are scriptural and covenantal. But they aren't Catholic. They can't be."

I suspected that Kimberly was secretly wondering just how scriptural Catholicism might be, but she wasn't about to share any such "doubts" with me. We had reached the point where we could hardly talk about anything without lapsing into a doctrinal quarrel; and yet most attempts to deal forthrightly with our differences would end in grief and frustration.

I encouraged Kimberly to eavesdrop on discussions I had with others about controversial aspects of Catholic doctrine. This indirect approach proved to be much less of a strain on our relationship than when we faced off alone.

To get away from the domestic strain and academic pressure, I taught a weekly Bible study at my parish, Saint Bernard's. Monsignor Bruskewitz was more than supportive—naturally, since it was his solid preaching that whetted the parishioners' appetite for more of the Bible. It was encouraging for me to see—and for Kimberly to hear about—their insatiable appetite for Scripture. What a privilege it was to open up God's Word to share the treasures of the Church's Faith with my new Catholic brothers and sisters. After finishing one particularly exciting session—on "A Biblical Explanation of Indulgences"—an older parishioner named Joe announced, "Yep, sometimes it takes an immigrant to explain it for the natives."

A few months after my reception into the Church, a plague of doubt descended upon me; not about whether I had done the wrong thing in becoming Catholic, but rather about whether I had committed professional suicide, leaving myself without any vocational options. After all, I thought, how can I shift from being a master of evangelical theology to serving as a lowly apprentice in Catholic dogma? Not that I wasn't enthralled with studying Catholic theology; it's just that I didn't see any practical way for it to put bread on our table.

I called up my father, in Pittsburgh, who was still running our family business, Helm and Hahn, a small company that designed and manufactured jewelry. A few years before, he had hired my older brother, Fritz. I was hoping that he might have an opening for some more family help.

"Dad, you wouldn't happen to have a job in the shop for an erstwhile evangelical theologian, would you?"

He paused and then spoke with a tone of deep regret. "Scotty, I'd love to have you work with us. You know that. But I wouldn't be able to hire you now. The economy here is weak and the jewelry trade is in a general slump across the country. We're having to trim down and tighten up everywhere. I'm so sorry, Son."

"It's all right, Dad. I was just hoping to find a job doing something to support my family."

"Scotty, what are you talking about? I distinctly remember hearing your college president say he wanted you back teaching theology there as soon as possible. And what about your professors at Gordon-Conwell? Didn't they tell you to pursue a doctorate so that you could return to teach there as well?"

"Yeah, Dad, but that was before I went Catholic. Now I'm *persona non grata* at both places. Neither one would even consider hiring a papist pariah like me."

"Scotty, I'm sorry to hear that. But there's one thing I'd still say, and that is, don't give up on theology yet. You've got a love for studying it and a gift for teaching it. If I were you, I would stick with it for a while longer."

Thank God for fatherly wisdom.

It was hitting me harder than ever before that here I had a growing family to support but no longer any craft with which to support them. It dawned on me that I might never have the time to master Latin, much less all the writings of Thomas Aquinas, Bonaventure, Cajetan, Bellarmine and a host of other worthies. How could I ever teach Catholic theology?

Help and consolation came from two sources. The first source was my previous undergraduate study of philosophy at Grove City College, where I had become enamored with and steeped in the philosophy of Saint Thomas. In spite of my anti-Catholic outlook, I had known a good thing when I found it, and, in my mind, no one could compare to Aquinas. I had naturally discounted anything distinctively Catholic in his writings. (Poor Thomas was born too soon, I thought, long before the light of Luther and Calvin could guide him.) But I had devoured his philosophical writings, especially his metaphysics, eventually acquiring the rather odd and unlikely reputation for being an "evangelical Thomist".

Consolation also came from a second source, namely, one kindly old priest and emeritus librarian at Saint Francis Seminary named Father Ray Fetterer, who took pity on a poor Presbyterian graduate student reading his way into the Church. Whenever a Catholic convent, monastery, college or high school would shut down in the region, their libraries would be sent down to Father

Fetterer at the archdiocesan seminary for sorting and stacking in an old basement gymnasium.

Tens of thousands of old books in theology, Scripture, philosophy, history and literature ended up on the shelves for interested folks to browse through and purchase at rock-bottom prices set by a philanthropic old priest. I discovered this gold mine by accident; it was not advertised and seldom open—usually by appointment only. Within a year's time, I had acquired literally scores of boxes of books; and since he felt such pity for my plight, I paid only a fraction of the already low prices that he usually charged. For me it was like a dream come true—by God's grace, a priest's beneficence and a convert's dumb luck!

For a few hundred dollars, then, I ended up with thousands of books, including such classics as the sixty-volume Blackfriars' edition of Saint Thomas Aquinas' *Summa Theologica* (in Latin and English), more than two dozen volumes of the *Works of John Henry Cardinal Newman*, the monumental *Dictionnaire de théologie catholique* in fifteen enormous volumes, the old *Catholic Encyclopedia*, the *New Catholic Encyclopedia*, along with hundreds of volumes of Scripture commentaries and patristic writings, not to mention several decades of expensive theological journals, such as *The Thomist, Theological Studies, Communio, American Ecclesiastical Review, Catholic Biblical Quarterly, Revue biblique, Biblica* and *Vetus Testamentum*. By God's grace, I found myself the owner of a personal library of Catholic theology, philosophy and history that a seminary would have been blessed to possess.

What was I to do with such a treasure—go into jewelry?

Instead, God used such consolations to restore my trust that he would make up for whatever I lacked in Catholic theological training. Besides, I discovered there really were no Catholic institutions at the time where a layman like me could receive orthodox doctrinal formation in the Catholic Tradition, even if I had had the time and money to afford it. Still I wondered whether or not there was a niche for me anywhere in the Church.

One evening I received a phone call from Dr. John Hittinger, a philosophy professor at the College of Saint Francis in Joliet, Illinois. He represented a search committee that was looking for a qualified theology professor to teach lower- and upper-division courses the following year, mostly to Catholic undergraduates.

I did not feel particularly qualified, nor had I even compiled a résumé yet, much less circulated one. Since I had not applied for this (or any other) position, I sat there wondering, as we chatted, where he had got my name. When I asked, he referred to a "reliable contact" in Marquette's theology department who had recommended me. I was surprised but grateful.

At the time, however, I was still hoping to spend the next year as a full-time student working to write and defend my doctoral thesis. But finances were so tight that I was already wondering if that were an affordable option. It was looking more and more doubtful; but even if it did work out, I could still use the experience of going through a job interview at a Catholic institution. Besides, John let me know that there were over thirty applicants for the job, so I figured, what were my chances anyway?

The interview went very well; they wanted me. Maybe it was my enthusiasm as a neophyte. In any case, the situation there was attractive. Here was an institution whose president was interested in restoring the Catholic identity of the college after it had been seriously diluted through years of financial, academic and spiritual pressures. It sounded like an exciting challenge. After a second interview and considerable prayer, I decided to accept the position.

At the time, Kimberly and our two boys were not attending Mass with me. Monsignor Bruskewitz said it would be permissible, under our unique set of circumstances, for me to accompany them to Elmbrook Church, so long as it didn't jeopardize my Catholic faith. I went simply to bring more peace to our Sundays.

One Sunday morning at Elmbrook, we were standing up, singing the closing hymn, when suddenly Kimberly turned to me, white as a ghost, and muttered, "Scott, something may be very wrong." She sat down beside me, dazed and half-conscious. As the congregation was leaving, Kimberly grabbed my hand, gripping it very tightly. "Scott, I'm bleeding—a lot." At this point, she was halfway through her third pregnancy.

I had her lie down on the pew, and, not knowing what else to do, I dashed to the pay phone and tried to reach our obstetrician. On a Sunday morning, what were my chances? Besides, he was brand new to the city. But that didn't keep me from praying—hard—to Saint Gerard and Saint Joseph.

The doctor's answering service wasn't sure where he was but would try to "beep" him. When I hung up, I felt close to despair. "Lord, why would you bring us to this point? Kimberly already feels abandoned by you as it is."

Less than two minutes later the pay phone rang. I picked it up, wondering who it could be. "Hello!?"

"Dr. Marmion here. May I speak to Scott Hahn?"

"Uh, yes, it's me, Dr. Marmion."

"Scott, what's wrong?"

"Kimberly is hemorrhaging badly."

"Scott, where are you?"

"We're outside of Milwaukee, in a town called Brookfield."

"Where in Brookfield?"

"At Elmbrook Church. It's pretty far out."

"Where are you in the church?"

"I'm right outside the sanctuary near the front doors."

"I'll be right up. I just happened to be visiting Elmbrook this morning—I'm right below you in the basement."

A half minute later Dr. Marmion was at Kimberly's side—just enough time for me to send off a couple of requests to Saint Gerard for his intercession. Dr. Marmion directed us to go immediately to Saint Joseph's Hospital, saying he would meet us there. Some close friends took our sons, and we raced off to the hospital.

Once there, we realized the Lord had spared our baby, and, with diligent care, the condition of "placenta previa" would not rob us of our child.

For the first time in a long while, we praised God together from the depths of our hearts.

Kimberly:

I tried to fit in to Scott's life as a Catholic. The week after Easter, Scott led a Bible study in our home and I sat in. When a young man was asked to open in prayer, he promptly led in a Hail Mary. I left the room in agony, fell on my knees in my bedroom and wept bitterly—how dare he say those words in my home, rubbing salt into my open wound from Scott's conversion! Later, I tried to rejoin them, but their comments and expressions of Catholic piety were overwhelming. Soon Scott moved the Bible study out of our home, for which I was most grateful.

Fortunately Scott never made the Catholic Faith a "submission issue" between us, forcing me to submit to his spiritual leadership when my heart could not yet yield to what my mind had not yet grasped. Though he yearned with his whole being to have me at his side at Mass, pleading with me to share his joy in the Church and assist him in ministry within the Church, he would not misuse his call to lead our family spiritually to require me to go against my conscience. In fact, he respected me for holding on to my convictions, though he challenged my continued unwillingness to look at the issues involved in our spiritual separation.

However, we both knew, and it was my deep conviction, that our children belonged to the Lord primarily under Scott's spiritual leadership. That meant that eventually, at some point in time, they would be raised Catholic, regardless of whether I was Protestant or Catholic. This was a tremendously painful realization—that I could be the lone Protestant in my family. I could hardly bear the thought of how isolated I would feel in that situation.

In fact, it briefly interfered with my deep desire for another child. I told Scott that I was unwilling simply to procreate more children for the Pope! Thankfully, in just a few weeks time, the Lord used my own desire for more children and my love for Scott to open my heart in yielding to the Lord's will regarding more children. I needed to be obedient to the Lord in being open to new life and to trust him with the consequences of the outcome of the children's ecclesiastical affiliation.

Usually Scott put his religious objects, such as Rosaries, scapulars and holy cards, in his drawer, but occasionally I would find them on the dresser. I noticed a certain jealousy developing in me toward Mary (similar to the jealousy I heard that men sometimes had toward Jesus when their wives became Christians). I was at a distinct disadvantage—she was supposedly pure, lovely, wonderful to be with, kind, compassionate; and, in contrast, I was not showing the same loving kindness toward Scott. He would go for a walk, and I knew it was to pray the Rosary with Mary. I was glad he was not going to do it in front of me; but I was jealous that he had time to walk and talk nicely to her but did not seem to have that kind of time for me.

One day when Scott was preparing to go share his testimony of how he became Catholic, I blurted out, "I cannot understand why God would take a well-trained young couple, committed to a common vision for life and ministry together, and totally change their lives around so that now we are going in completely different directions. Why would he do that?"

I wasn't ready for Scott's reply. Scott said to me, "Is it possible that God loves us so much? Since, on your own, you never would have been interested in studying the Catholic Faith, perhaps he's converted me first, and had me go through terrible loneliness—isolated from many Protestants, Catholics on campus who really don't care what I did, and definitely the loneliness between the two of us—all so he could gradually show you the beauty of the Catholic Church? So that he could gather you in? So that he could bless you with the sacraments? So that he could give you the fullness of the faith you already possess?"

I said, "It's awfully hard to see how that is love, but I guess that's possible." I had to admit I certainly would never have looked at the Catholic Church on my own.

I added, "Just don't expect me to go running around giving my testimony, if I do join."

To which Scott quickly responded, "I wouldn't want you to convert until you couldn't wait to share your testimony." With that, he was out the door, and I was left alone with my thoughts again.

The waves of grief engulfed us separately as we contemplated the death of many dreams. I know grief may sound like too strong an emotion to attach to this, but I really don't know a better word. We were both undergoing a slow death but were very unsure if there ever would be a kind of resurrection. Scott at least had the consolation of believing that he was following the will of God. I did not have that kind of certainty.

My grief differed from Scott's. I had sorrow for the loss of ever again being a pastor's wife, something which had been a lifelong dream. I did not see where I could fit in to a call for Scott to train priests, which he now stated he wanted to do; we had wanted to counsel young couples getting married, which did not happen in a Catholic seminary.

The possibility of returning to either Grove City College or Gordon-Conwell Theological Seminary to teach, a dream we both had had, was now gone. The future was uncertain as to whether or not Scott would ever get to teach at the level for which he had trained.

I had always desired all my children to go into full-time Christian service, but now I realized that if they did that I would have to suffer the loss of grandchildren. (As Protestants, my father, uncle, brother and husband were married ministers, so celibacy had never before been an issue.)

And, small as it may seem, I dreaded the possibility of our home becoming cluttered with religious paraphernalia. When one friend gave us a crucifix in front of a group of people, I could not even speak. In my heart all I could think was, You have my spouse; but don't redecorate my house!

Thankfully Scott reached over and, taking it, said, "I know right where I'll put this in my study." Our dear friends had no idea of what pain that caused. And there was no way to share it so it could be lessened.

There were no more deep theological conversations without their becoming gut-wrenching exchanges. Scott had been my best friend, with whom I could have shared my burden of sorrow. But now how could I do this, when *he* was the very one causing much of it? And Scott's loneliness could have been borne more easily had I been at his side, but I could not and would not help him shoulder it—after all, it had been his choice, and these were the consequences.

Scott suffered tremendous loneliness. He was misunderstood and rejected by many Protestant friends who didn't want to talk to him for the same reasons I didn't want to talk to him. (Some friends hung in there with us until I converted; then they, too, rejected our overtures of friendship.) He felt that former professors didn't think he was worth pursuing to convince him he was wrong. And he couldn't understand the nonchalance of a number of Catholics at Marquette over his conversion, acting rather ho-hum over the whole thing, rather than welcoming him for all he had risked and left behind. And he had begun living as a Catholic in a Protestant family, going to Mass alone (which he did for two and a half years) and not sharing his Faith's distinctiveness with the children because the agreed-to timing of that had not yet come.

The loneliness between us was excruciating. We had had such a close friendship, sharing so much of life. While in seminary, plenty of wives couldn't have cared less what their husbands were studying, any more than they would have wanted to understand balance sheets and tax laws if their husbands were tax accountants. But I had come alongside him, studied with him, wrestled with texts with him and learned from him. Now, instead of sharing his discoveries and rejoicing with him, I dreaded hearing details. And I chose not to read his papers carefully, though I typed them for him. (If you type fast enough, you don't have to read the text.) How could Scott share his burden of sorrow with me, when *I* was the very one causing much of it?

The Bible was my only consolation. But I began to be concerned about even picking up the Scriptures, because Scott kept telling me that the Bible said something different from what I thought. Scott claimed the Bible had led him to the Catholic Faith. But the Bible was the basis of my faith!

Once, he threw out to me, "What's the pillar and foundation of truth?"

My quick reply was "The Word of God".

He then said, "Why does Saint Paul say, in 1 Timothy 3:15, it's the Church? Why doesn't that answer come to Protestant minds?"

"That's just in your Catholic Bible, Scott."

Then he opened my Bible and showed me that verse, which I did not remember ever reading before.

We did not have simple conversations about theology. We had debates about theology. Sometimes we would discuss things until two or three A.M., and over breakfast next morning, Scott wondered if I had any new thoughts! We would discuss theology, trying to keep our discussion cordial, and then it would get very painful and difficult. So we would have to stop, back off and go into our own corners for a while. It was a separate grief.

Some friends counseled me that a wife should submit to her husband no matter what her brain says—they did not understand why I would not go ahead and convert. Other Protestant friends continually reminded me they were praying that I could hang on until Scott came around. And there were Catholics who thought, What's the big deal? So Mary bothers you; you'll get over it.

Scott was stuck with me because he did not believe in divorce. Actually, I didn't either. When we married, we agreed that we would never even joke about the term—we felt so deeply about it. And yet there were two different times in that initial year, following Scott's conversion, when I walked around our block and asked myself, Can I leave him? I thought of what hotel I would go to, and what I would do, because I couldn't face the pain of this grief. I did not think I could cope with the pain—physically my heart hurt, and emotionally I was devastated. All I could think of was escape.

But I knew I could not leave Scott without leaving God as well. And to leave God, I knew, would be to consign myself to hell. The existence of both God and hell was too great for me to follow through with walking away, thanks be to God. So, within ten minutes, God gave me enough grace to endure ten more. Then I was able to stay and endure longer.

This passage from Lamentations 3 best captures the agony in my heart and my struggle to regain hope in the Lord:

> He drove into my heart the arrows of his quiver. He made my teeth grind on gravel and made me cower in ashes. My soul is bereft of peace. I have forgotten what happiness is. So I say, "Gone is my glory and my expectation from the Lord." Remember my affliction and my bitterness, the wormwood and the gall. My soul continually thinks of it and is bowed down within me. But this I call to mind and therefore I have hope: the steadfast love of the Lord never ceases, his mercies never come to an end. They are new every morning. Great is thy faithfulness. The Lord is my portion, says my soul, therefore I will hope in him.

Somehow there was hope—not because of Scott or me, but because of the faithfulness of God. Somehow the Lord would make his mercies new to me—and to Scott—every day for us to get the grace we would need during this very difficult time of need.

Scott was relishing things Catholic (although he was not flaunting them). He was crossing himself in prayer. He had a crucifix in his office. I overheard him say a Hail Mary with a friend. Each one of those things was a stab in my heart. Each one was another reminder of the disunity we had.

The lack of the joy of my salvation was very intense for me. And it was made especially painful at times because I could tell how much joy he was suppressing. Even in the midst of his pain, he really did have the joy of the Lord in new ways, especially in regard to the Eucharist. Repeatedly in my prayer journal I was asking the Lord, Where is the joy of my salvation? I know I'm saved. Scott doesn't even question that, but where is the joy, and why is his so strong?

I was very recalcitrant—that's the best word to use. I wanted to want to study, but I was fearful of it at the same time. He would come down and say, "Kimberly, would you just read a paragraph of an article?"

"Is it about Mary?"

"Yes."

"No. Please go away. Can't you find common ground for us to read and talk about?"

A knowledgeable and conversant convert is not an easy person to live with. (I may not have read much, but I heard enough theology to earn another Master's.) For him, having a close-minded person, unwilling to converse, was very difficult.

The hardest thing of all at this time was not understanding where God was, because I could not tell if God was rooting for Scott or for me. After an evening of pouring my heart out to God with many tears, I wrote this "conversation" with God in my prayer journal:

> "Are you in heaven, irritated at this prolonged emotional tantrum, or are you weeping with me, Lord? Are you holding me at this time, or are you tugging at me to pull me onward? I don't want to pit you, Lord, against Scott or against me, but where are you in all of this?"

> "I'm on the Cross suffering for the very sins you both are now committing. I am the ascended and seated Lord of all who is calling you to a marriage that exemplifies me and my Church."

> "Can we do that, Lord, in a mixed marriage?"

"No, that cannot be my will."

"What is your will, O Lord, and how can we follow your will in the midst of discovering your will? How can we grow the most in this suffering, Lord? Can I be loyal to Scott, to friends and to family? To whom can I speak my sorrow? Please restore to me the joy of my salvation. May I praise you as long as I live. Be pleased, O God, to heal my wounds and restore me. Please strengthen Scott during this time of suffering and lead him in the ways of truth."

Despair was constantly at the doorstep. Scott has always said my biggest fault is being pathologically positive. But during this time, despair was something that I struggled with tremendously. Some of the crosses we bore at that time we had hewn for ourselves; some we had hewn for each other.

When a Catholic friend prayed over me, she said the word she received from the Lord was that we were being given an "apostolate of the broken Body of Christ". The anguish we were experiencing in our marriage was similar to the sadness and the rending that happened through the Reformation and other schisms—God was giving us a precious gift that might last only a brief time. We needed to try to grasp that as something good. I had no idea if that was God's plan, but we certainly felt, on a daily basis, the brokenness brought to families ever since the Reformation. And we shared the pain of that separation.

Activism became a bond that greatly helped us to work together. Fighting abortion and pornography side by side gave us common goals and strengthened our marriage both through ministering together and growing in friendships together. It helped us to have some outward focus when the inward focus was too painful.

Christmas 1986 we found out that we had another child on the way. The word the Lord gave me was "child of reconciliation". I kept saying, "O God, does this mean that she's going to be Catholic? Does that mean I'm going to have to be Catholic?" I immediately began to pray.

My next thought was, How was this child to be baptized? This was a crisis—I believed in infant baptism, but I was attending a nondenominational church that did not. I had always dreamed of my dad baptizing our babies, but I did not see how that was possible. And yet to have the child baptized Catholic seemed an admission that she belonged to the Catholic Church.

It was very difficult. I kept much of this struggle within me—Scott and I never really discussed it. God was very gracious to guide my heart apart from arguments with Scott. In recognition of Scott as the spiritual leader of our home, it seemed fitting to yield my heart to having the baby baptized Catholic. Finally, I had a real peace about it and about knocked Scott's socks off when I calmly asked him to make arrangements with Monsignor Bruskewitz for baptism once the child was born.

Right before our daughter was born, I had an important conversation with my father. My father is one of the godliest men I know. He has truly been the father I have needed to lead me to my heavenly Father. My dad could sense sadness in my voice.

He asked, "Kimberly, do you pray the prayer I pray every day? Do you say, 'Lord, I'll go wherever you want me to go, do whatever you want me to do, say whatever you want me to say and give away whatever you want me to give away'?"

"No, Dad, I don't pray that prayer these days." He had no idea of the agony I was enduring over Scott's being Catholic.

He said, genuinely shocked, "You don't!"

"Dad, I'm afraid to. I'm afraid if I prayed that prayer, that could mean joining the Roman Catholic Church. And I will never become a Roman Catholic!"

"Kimberly, I don't believe it will mean you will become a Roman Catholic. What it means is that Jesus Christ is either Lord of your entire life, or he isn't Lord at all. You don't tell God where you will and won't go. What you tell him is, you're yielded to him. That's what matters most to me, far more than whether or not you become a Roman Catholic. Otherwise you are in the process of hardening your heart toward the Lord. If you can't pray that prayer, pray for the grace to pray that prayer until you can. Yield your heart to him—you can trust him."

He risked a lot saying that.

For thirty days I prayed every day, "God, give me the grace to pray that prayer." I was so afraid that by praying that prayer, it would seal my fate—I would have to throw away my brain, forget my heart and follow Scott like a moron into the Catholic Church.

Finally, I was ready to pray that prayer, trusting God with the consequences. What I found out was, I was the one who had made the cage, and, instead of locking it, the Lord opened the door to set me free. My heart leapt. Now I was free to begin to want to study and to probe, to begin to explore things with a measure of joy once again. Now I could say, Okay, God, it isn't the way I planned my life, but your dreams are good enough for me. What do you want to do in my heart? in my marriage? in our family? I wanted to know.

On August 7, 1987, Hannah Lorraine was born. It was with great joy we welcomed our first daughter into the world, and with great relief that the placenta previa condition and intermittent bleeding trauma were over. This baby was another living symbol of the power of prayer and a witness to our abiding love even in the midst of great pain and struggle.

I went to Hannah's baptism not even knowing if the priest were going to say, "Mrs. Hahn, would you please sit over there while I baptize your child over here." All I knew was that, in obedience to God, she needed to be baptized Catholic.

From the moment we walked in, Monsignor Bruskewitz welcomed me and cordially invited me to do and say all that in good conscience I could do and say. Though I kept silent during the invocation of saints and disagreed in my heart with his explanation of baptism, I was astounded at the beauty of the liturgy. I participated as wholeheartedly as I could.

I was not prepared for the beauty of the baptismal liturgy. It was everything I would have prayed for for my daughter! At one point, right after the priest had finished praying an incredible prayer for our child to hear and respond to the Gospel, I was squeezing Scott's hand from the sheer joy of the moment. (He feared I was clutching him so I would not run out.)

Then Monsignor concluded that prayer, "Amen and Amen."

I blurted out, "Amen!" I could not hold it in. (That may be typical for a Baptist, but I was raised Presbyterian!) We all laughed together. And Monsignor assured me the sentiments were shared by all.

I did not feel as though Hannah had been bound and

chained by the burden of being a Roman Catholic (as at one time I had feared), but rather, she was being freed to be the child of God she was created to be. As I left Saint Bernard's church that day, God was doing an important work inside of me. I said to Scott, "I know today is a turning point for me." It wasn't the only one, but it was an important one.

8

A Rome-antic Reunion

Scott:

Shortly before moving to Joliet, Kimberly and I bought our first house just three blocks away from the College of Saint Francis. We moved there less than a month after Kimberly had given birth to Hannah in Milwaukee. She was still recovering from her third Caesarian section, while I had just finished up my language requirements by passing the French and German exams. In the midst of it all, I had to prepare the four courses that I would be teaching in less than two weeks.

Working with college students proved to be exciting and rewarding. I quickly learned that very few, if any, of my Catholic students really understood their Faith, even the basics. I got a special kick out of helping "cradle Catholics" discover the riches of their own heritage, especially from Scripture. I started a weekly Bible study with a dozen members of the football team and spent a lot of time with students outside of class. Living three blocks from the college proved to be a real boon for building relationships.

In three years, I also discovered that it takes more than the sincere desire of a few members of the administration and faculty to restore the Catholic identity of a college that has traveled a long way down the road of secularization. It was a real struggle at times. It was my first direct exposure to Catholics who had abandoned their Faith but who would not relinquish their positions of power. Fortunately, I was privileged to work in a department with four great colleagues: John Hittinger, Greg Sobolewski, Sister Rose Marie Surwillo and Dan Hauser.

One day at work I got a phone call from Bill Bales, one of my ex-friends from seminary, who had become a Presbyterian pastor in Virginia. He was calling to apologize for something he'd done when Kimberly and the kids spent a week visiting with them, apart from me, almost a year before.

Bill spoke in a quiet and contrite tone. "Scott, I need to ask your forgiveness."

"What for, Bill? I'm just glad you're still willing to talk with me!"

"Scott, I'm afraid that you might not be willing to talk with me after I tell you what I did."

He could not have done more to pique my curiosity and suspicion. "Okay, Bill, what did you do?"

"A few months ago your wife went through your Catholic arguments with me; I think she was hoping that I would give her lots of ammunition to shoot them down. I really wasn't ready with answers. Instead, I counseled her to consider whether or not she had biblical grounds to divorce you."

His words hit me hard; but I was so glad to be back on speaking terms that I quickly recovered. "That's all right, Bill. As you know, if it'd been me five years ago, I would have *urged* divorce in the same situation."

Then Bill paused and drew his breath. "There's something else, Scott."

I wasn't sure I was ready for a second salvo so soon. "Uh, what is it, Bill?"

"Well, I told Kimberly that I'd get back to her with solid arguments to refute your Catholic ideas."

"Yeah, go on."

"Well, it has been quite a while, and I haven't come up with a single one."

I was barely able to suppress my triumphant tone. "Bill, that's a forgivable offense if ever there was one."

"Thanks, Scott, but I'm not apologizing for that. I'm calling to ask you for help. During the last few months I've been doing a lot of thinking and reading about the Catholic Faith, and I have several issues and questions that I'd like to talk over with you."

Immediately I realized what he was saying. "Bill, just tell me this, are you feeling the force of the biblical arguments for the Catholic Faith?"

"You could say that."

"Are you also feeling a certain amount of terror as you ponder the long-term implications for you as a Presbyterian pastor?"

"You better believe it."

By then I had figured out the real reason for his call. It became the first of many. Over the next year, Bill would call with questions based on his own intensive reading of Catholic theology. In my mind, Bill was a special case. At seminary he went beyond all of us in his understanding and love of Hebrew. He taped photocopied pages of the Hebrew Bible to the walls in his study just to help with studying and memorizing it.

After graduation Bill went into the Presbyterian ministry, serving as an associate pastor under Jack Lash, my closest ex-friend from seminary. Bill was still a minister there when he called me. Back in the good old days, when I was still a Calvinist, Jack had me preach at his ordination and installation service. Since I had become a Catholic, he would not speak to me.

After months of study and periodic phone debates, Bill's direction was becoming clear. His research was leading him closer and closer to Rome. Jack and the church elders took steps to counteract his potential defection. At times it got mean and nasty. This only intensified his wife's resolve to study Catholicism more fairly. As a result, both of them, along with Kimberly, kept reading and talking more and more.

Up to this point, my confrontational tactics with Kimberly had not accomplished anything constructive. Attempts to engage her in debate were fruitless. Any books I would recommend were thereby sealed with a kiss of death. God was trying to teach me to back off so that the Holy Spirit might have more room to operate.

Instead of offering apologetic arguments, I went back to sharing my personal feelings; not, however, as an alternate strategy by which I could maneuver and manipulate her more effectively. It was simply the only respectful and loving way to deal with our differences. I gradually accepted the fact that Kimberly might never become a Catholic; nor was her conversion to be my perennial project.

After moving in and making some new friends in the community, Kimberly and I began encountering the toughest brand of anti-Catholic either of us had ever come across before, the ex-Catholic fundamentalist. Unlike typical anti-Catholic Protestants, who enjoy nothing more than intense biblical debates over Catholic issues like Mary and the Pope, the ex-Catholic fundamentalists we would run into were filled with such rage and resentment toward the Church that it rendered them incapable of rational discourse. To them I was demon-possessed, so they urged Kimberly not even to listen, since Satan was using me to lure her with his lies. With an independent and intelligent woman like Kimberly, that advice was bound to backfire.

Most of the time, I looked forward to conversations with anti-Catholic fundamentalists who were concerned for my salvation. I appreciated their evangelistic zeal.

One night at dinner, I related to Kimberly a conversation I had had earlier that day with a fundamentalist who, upon learning that I was Catholic, went right to work on evangelizing me.

Of course, he started by asking, "Have you been born again?"

I replied, "Yes, indeed I have. But what do *you* mean by it?"

He look puzzled. "Have you accepted Jesus Christ as your personal Lord and Savior?"

I smiled broadly and said, "Yes, indeed I have. But that's not why I'm born again. I'm born again because of what Christ did through the Holy Spirit when I was baptized."

He still looked stumped, so I continued. "You see, the Bible nowhere states, 'You must accept Jesus Christ as your personal Lord and Savior.' It's a great thing to do, but it's not what our Lord was talking about when he told Nicodemus in John 3:3 that he had to be 'born again'. Jesus clarified what he *did* mean when he said just two verses later, 'You must be born of water and the Spirit', which he stated with reference to baptism. John made that point clear to the reader, because as soon as he finished describing Jesus' discourse with Nicodemus in verses 2–21, he stated in the very next verse that 'After

this Jesus and his disciples went into the land of Judea;
there he remained with them and baptized'. And a few
verses later, John reported how 'the Pharisees had heard
that Jesus was making and baptizing more disciples than
John.' In other words, when Jesus said that we must be
'born again', what he meant was baptism."

I freely admitted to Kimberly that I might have come
on too strong. I went on to explain why I thought it was
wrong for fundamentalists to assume that Catholics aren't
really Christians just because they don't use certain biblical phrases in the same way; especially when fundamentalists don't even interpret those phrases properly in their
original context. She completely agreed.

Shortly after that, I came back from attending a conference for theologians at Franciscan University of Steubenville. It was the first time that I had visited there. I
was amazed to have met so many orthodox Catholics
with such evangelical zeal. I was even more astonished
by what I saw during the noon Mass: the chapel was
packed with hundreds of students who were singing
their hearts out, with a great love for Christ in the Holy
Eucharist.

I could hardly wait to tell Kimberly about it. She was
thrilled to hear that the evangelical zeal she grew up with
could find a home in the Catholic Church.

I told a friend in my parish about the ongoing struggle
to share the Catholic Faith with my evangelical wife. I described the enthusiastic singing, the dynamic biblical
preaching and the warm fellowship—all of which Kimberly had experienced since childhood. He made a curious suggestion. "Scott, personally I think Protestants have
all those things because they don't have the Blessed Sacrament. Once you have the Real Presence of Christ in the

Holy Eucharist, you don't need all the rest. Don't you agree?"

I bit my tongue. I did not want to react, but I needed to correct what I took to be a disturbing oversight. "I think I know what you're trying to say, that eucharistic worship can be quiet and reverent without losing any depth or power. I agree with that. In fact, I'm coming to a real appreciation for Gregorian Chant and Latin in the liturgy; but I would say it differently. I would rather say that because we *do* have Christ's Real Presence in the Holy Eucharist, then we—even more than Protestants— have something to sing about, to preach about and to celebrate together."

There was awkward silence for a moment. "Yeah, who can disagree when you put it that way?"

Wondering out loud, I said, "But why is it that we don't always put it that way?"

He had no answer; nor did I.

I have always wondered why so many Catholics never delve more deeply into the mysteries of their Faith. It has always amazed me to discover how each and every mystery is grounded in Scripture, centered on Christ and somehow preserved and proclaimed in the liturgy of the Church, the covenant family of God.

This really came home to me one day after I attended the Mass on All Souls' Day. Kimberly wanted to know the significance of the feast. In no time at all, the conversation was deteriorating into another debate over the doctrine of Purgatory. I decided to transpose the doctrine into a major key, so to speak, by framing it in terms of God's covenant love.

"Kimberly, the Bible shows how many times God revealed himself in fire to his people in order to renew his covenant with them: as a 'fire pot and flaming torch' with Abraham in Genesis 15; in the burning bush with Moses in Exodus 3; in the pillar of fire with Israel in Numbers 9; in the heavenly fire which consumed the altar sacrifices with Solomon and Elijah in 1 Kings 8 and 18; in the 'tongues of fire' with the apostles at Pentecost in Acts 2. . . . "

Kimberly interrupted, "All right, Scott, what's your point?"

I had one chance to get it right. "Simply this. When Hebrews 12:29 describes God as 'a consuming fire', it isn't necessarily referring to his anger. There's the fire of hell, but there's an infinitely hotter fire in heaven; it's God himself. So fire refers to God's infinite love even more than his eternal wrath. God's nature is like a raging inferno of fiery love. In other words, heaven must be hotter than hell.

"No wonder Scripture refers to the angels who are closest to God as the Seraphim, which literally means 'the burning ones' in Hebrew. That's also why Saint Paul can describe in 1 Corinthians 3:13 how all the saints must pass through a fiery judgment in which 'each man's work will become manifest; for the Day will disclose it, because it will be revealed with fire. . . . '

"Clearly, he's not talking about the fire of hell, since they're saints who are being judged. He's talking about a fire that prepares them for eternal life with God in heaven; so the purpose of the fire is manifest: to reveal whether their works are pure ('gold and silver') or impure ('wood, hay and straw').

"Verse 15 makes it clear that some saints who are destined for heaven will pass through fire and suffer: 'If any man's work is burned up, he will suffer loss, though he himself will be saved, but only as through fire.' The fire is there for the purpose of purging saints. That means it is a purgatorial fire; one that purifies and prepares the saints to be enveloped in the consuming fire of God's loving presence forever."

I had said a lot; perhaps too much. I sat there waiting for Kimberly to react with anger and frustration, as she had every other time I had raised the subject of Purgatory. Instead, she sat there, quiet, with a thoughtful expression on her face. I could tell by her eyes that she was pondering what she had heard. I decided not to push it any farther—for once.

In the middle of the fall '89 semester, I got a call out of the blue from Pat Madrid of Catholic Answers, which I knew to be the finest Catholic apologetics organization in the country. Based in San Diego, Catholic Answers was founded by Karl Keating, author of *Catholicism and Fundamentalism*, the book I found more useful than any other for helping people answer the fundamentalist attacks against the Church. It was good finally to connect with such kindred spirits.

We stayed in close touch for the next few weeks. As I talked with them about future job possibilities, they expressed interest in flying me out for an informal interview and having me do an evening seminar for them at Saint Francis de Sales Church in Riverside, California. The arrangements were then made.

After my three and a half years of searching out like-minded souls, my meeting with Karl and Pat felt like an oasis. Saturday afternoon at the Catholic Answers office, I hastily typed an outline of the talk I would give for the evening seminar. It was to be an hour-long testimony of my conversion to the Catholic Faith, followed by questions and answers. The talk was similar to one I had given a dozen times before; but this time it turned out to be different from any other. It was to become "The Tape" (otherwise known as "Protestant Minister Becomes Catholic").

Ten minutes before I started, I was introduced to Terry Barber of Saint Joseph Communications, who was hastily assembling some tape-recording equipment for my talk. As he set up the microphone, he explained to me how he and his brand-new bride, Danielle, had just arrived back from their honeymoon in Fatima, Portugal. He also explained his lateness; he had recorded talks at five separate locations that day. Terry made it seem it was a last-minute decision even to show up for my talk. At the time, it didn't really matter to me; later on, we were both eternally grateful.

At 7:30 sharp, I was introduced to a small group of thirty-five people. After talking for over an hour—I have never ended anything on time—I took a short break and got back up for the Q & A session. When it was all over, I walked toward the back to talk with Pat.

While we were talking, Terry Barber came running up waving a copy of a cassette tape. "God is going to use this tape, my friend, I just know it."

I was pleased to see him so excited, but since I had given the same talk on so many other occasions when it had been taped, I did not think anything of it. I even thought to myself: How unprepared I was tonight; other times it was much better. Maybe that's why our Lord chose to use this particular talk in such a powerful way—since no one could take any of the credit but him.

I flew back home to Joliet and told Kimberly all about the weekend with Catholic Answers. I never bothered to tell her about the evening seminar. It still didn't seem all that significant. I was back to teaching my classes the next day.

A few weeks passed before I heard again from Terry Barber. He phoned to tell me that he had been sending out dozens of free copies of the tape to various Catholic leaders and groups across the country. Terry reported that he was getting a wonderful response.

Little did I know; that tape would change both of our lives—and one of our wives!

"No wonder", I said. "What would you expect from such entrepreneurial effort? Terry, I think you have the determination of an apostle."

I discovered that a copy had been sent to Catholic evangelist Father Ken Roberts, who listened to it and immediately ordered five thousand copies, which he then began distributing around the country. Father Ken's mention of the tape over EWTN opened the way for me to appear as a guest on "Mother Angelica, Live" several months later.

Karl and Pat both warned me. "Scott, very shortly your life is going to speed up and get very busy."

They were right; they were also partly to blame. One of our first cooperative ventures came shortly after "The Tape" was made. Catholic Answers sponsored a three-hour public debate between me and Dr. Robert Knudsen, Professor of Systematic Theology and Apologetics at Westminster Theological Seminary. During the first half of the evening, we debated *sola scriptura*; for the second half, *sola fide*. I have to confess to feeling more than a little fear in preparing to debate a world-class scholar on the two momentous issues dividing Protestants and Catholics.

I never dreamed of such a positive outcome. Not only did the Westminster Seminary students in attendance express their surprise and excitement at the end, but, what was more important, as soon as I returned home, Kimberly turned on a cassette player to listen to the entire debate. Three hours later, she sat there staring in stunned amazement. All she could say was, "I can't believe what I've just heard."

I was thrilled. I wasted no time, handing her a copy of "The Tape". It was the first time she had heard my testimony since I had become a Catholic.

Things kept speeding up. I got a call from Dr. Alan Schreck, then chairman of the theology department at Franciscan University of Steubenville. He told me about an opening in the department for the following academic year, 1990–1991, and suggested that I send him my résumé. I wasted no time in sending it off.

A couple of years before, Franciscan University had sponsored a conference on marriage and the family. I went out with Phil Sutton, a good friend and colleague who was teaching psychology at the College of Saint Francis at the time. Following the conference, during our drive home, we recalled how Jewish people around the world have a saying, "Next year in Jerusalem." Jokingly, Phil and I developed a new Catholic saying for ourselves, "Next year in Steubenville." The following year Phil left the College of Saint Francis to begin teaching at Franciscan University of Steubenville; he was hired to start their M.A. program in counseling. Now I was being considered the following year. Little had we known that the Lord would interpret a cute saying as a prayer.

When I told Kimberly about the opportunity, I reminded her of my experience at worship there. I told her about the university's pro-life commitment, from their president, Father Michael Scanlan, down to the faculty and students. I informed her that Franciscan University had more than a hundred students majoring in theology—more than Catholic University or Notre Dame—plus a Master of Arts program in theology, with a concentration in marriage and family. For the first time in more than five years, we were praying again with one heart.

Over Christmas we drove to Steubenville for the initial interview with Father Scanlan and Dr. Schreck. The day before we left, Kimberly suffered a second miscarriage. I was crushed, she was devastated. Near the end of his interview with both of us, Kimberly told him about what had just happened. She then asked him—a Catholic priest!—to pray over her. Without a moment's hesitation, he stood up and walked out from behind his desk, placed his hands upon her shoulders and began to call down the healing grace of God in prayer.

During the interview, Father Scanlan shared about his own struggles in the past with certain Marian doctrines and devotions. Nothing could have pleased Kimberly more than to hear how it took effort for a Catholic priest to grow in his understanding and appreciation of Mary. She listened attentively as he went on to explain his recent discovery of how biblical and Christ-centered Marian doctrine and devotion really are, once they're properly understood and practiced as Vatican II presented them. It was brief but effective.

Several weeks went by before I flew out for a second interview and to give a lecture to the student body. Both went very well. My time with Alan and Nancy Schreck was especially cordial. Besides being gracious hosts, they were becoming good friends. Within days of returning home, we heard back from Alan that I had been offered the job. By then our prayers for divine guidance were anything but neutral. We eagerly accepted the offer.

Oddly enough, I was less sure than ever about where Kimberly stood on Catholic issues. I was finally learning the lesson drilled into my head by Gil Kaufmann, a good friend in Opus Dei: Beef up the romance and back off the doctrine.

I flew out to California to speak at a national conference on apologetics sponsored by Catholic Answers. Many people there had heard "The Tape" and were asking all about Kimberly. After I had finished the lecture, my first question went something like this: "Scott, we've all heard the tape you made a few months ago; tell us how your wife is doing in her struggle with the Catholic Faith." It was embarrassing; I had to tell them that I didn't know.

Later in the evening, I gave Kimberly a call at the Schrecks' home in Steubenville, where she was staying for the weekend while looking for housing. When I told her about all the people at the conference who had listened to the tape and how they wanted to find out where she was in her thinking, I asked if there was anything she would want me to say. I was hardly prepared for her answer.

After a pause, she said, "Tell them that when I was driving out to Steubenville yesterday, on Ash Wednesday, after much thought and prayer, it became clear that God was calling me to come home this Easter."

Neither of us could speak for over a minute. Then the tears, the prayers and the rejoicing began.

In a short time, everyone at the conference knew.

Kimberly was to be received at Saint Patrick's Church in Joliet during the Easter Vigil, 1990. (The timing seemed more than a little ironic; five years before, 1990 had been set as the earliest date for me to join the Church—my date became hers.) The joy of anticipating Kimberly's reception was overwhelming at times; it made entering the penitential spirit of Lent a unique challenge for both of us. Our celebration of Holy Week had never been so special.

In the middle of Holy Week, I happened to ask Kimberly in a rather off-handed way, "Whom have you chosen for your patron saint?"

She gave me a funny look. "What are you talking about?"

So I explained. "When you get confirmed, you have the opportunity to choose a 'confirmation name' that is typically taken from a 'patron saint' to whom you might feel close. For instance, when I joined the Church, I chose Saint Francis de Sales."

Kimberly still did not seem to be catching on. She asked, "Why him?"

I dutifully explained. "Saint Francis de Sales happened to be the Bishop of Geneva, Switzerland, while John Calvin was leading the people farther away from the Catholic Faith. I discovered through my reading that Saint Francis de Sales was such an effective preacher and apologist that, through his sermons and pamphlets, over forty thousand Calvinists were brought back into the Church. So I figured if he could guide all of them back then, he could guide one more back now. Besides, Saint Francis de Sales was also declared to be Patron of the Catholic Press, and since I owned around fifteen thousand books, I figured he was the natural choice for me."

Kimberly turned away with a somewhat wistful look. "I'll just have to pray about it, I guess, and see if the Lord brings anyone to mind."

I did not tell her, but I already knew who my first choice for her patron saint was. Two years before, shortly after joining the Church, I had attended a conference of the Fellowship of Catholic Scholars, where I met a well-known theologian, Germain Grisez. I sat with him and his wife, Jeannette, at the Saturday evening banquet. I shared with them all about the excitement of my conversion as well as my heartache over Kimberly's resistance.

At the end of our time together, they both looked at each other and then at me. Germain spoke up. "We know just what to do."

I did not catch the meaning behind his rather cryptic remark. I asked, "What do you mean by that?"

They both began telling me about Saint Elizabeth Ann Seton: housewife, mother of five children, Catholic convert from Protestantism and foundress of the American Sisters of Charity. She had recently been canonized as the first native-born American saint. They also mentioned that her shrine was near their home in Emmitsburg, Maryland.

Hearing them speak about Saint Elizabeth Ann Seton was interesting, but it did not strike me as the highlight of the conference—until later.

Within a week I received a package in the mail. Seeing "Germain and Jeannette Grisez" on the return address, I suspected some kind of Catholic paraphernalia, so I took it up to my study for opening, far away from Kimberly's anxious gaze. Inside was a copy of Joseph Dirvin's biography of Saint Elizabeth Ann Seton and something I had never seen before: a small reliquary, containing a relic of Mother Seton.

I had no idea what to do with the reliquary, so I asked a Catholic friend to explain it to me. After that, I began carrying the relic in my pocket. It served as a reminder, whenever things got tense between Kimberly and me, to commit her cause to the Lord through the patronage and intercession of Mother Seton.

One day the inevitable happened; while going through my pockets when doing the laundry, Kimberly found the reliquary.

"Scott, what in the world is this?"

I froze. With a poorly disguised nervous tone, I stammered, "Oh, nothing, Kimberly, it's really nothing. You don't want to know."

She looked at it suspiciously for a moment—I could tell she was afraid that if she asked any more, I'd probably explain something that she did not really care to hear about—so she handed it back to me.

With a combination of prudence and fear, I stopped carrying the reliquary around with me, placing it in the back of my desk drawer instead. By then I had buried the biography somewhere on the bottom shelf in a dark corner of my study.

I realize now that I probably should not have been surprised two years later—but I was.

The day after I had asked Kimberly about her confirmation name and patron saint, as I was getting ready for bed I asked, "What's that you're reading, Kimberly?"

"It's a book about Saint Elizabeth Ann Seton."

I stopped in the middle of putting on my pajamas. "Kimberly, may I ask, where did you find that?"

With a tone of nonchalance, she explained: "Well, Scott, I was rummaging through all your books today, and I happened to pull out this one."

I ignored the chills running up and down my spine. "Well, what do you think of it?"

"Oh, my," she said excitedly, "I've been reading about her for hours now, Scott, and I think I've found my patron saint."

Or she found you, I thought.

All I could do was mutter, "Oh, really." (I was no longer sure, at that point, where the "communion of saints" left off and the twilight zone began.) Then I sat down on the bed and explained to her what had happened some two years earlier. Afterward I gave her the relic.

We ended the day with a short prayer of thanks to God—and to his wonderful daughter, our spiritual sister-in-Christ, Saint Elizabeth Ann Seton.

The momentous evening finally arrived. Kimberly left for the Easter Vigil Mass a half hour early so Father Memenas could hear her first confession.

In the middle of the Mass, Kimberly handed me a note. I looked down and read the following lines: "Dearest Scott, I am *so* thankful for you and for your forging this path for us. I love you. K." I was too numb with joy to say anything; but the smile and the tears were enough for Kimberly to know what I was thinking.

We shared the Eucharist together for the first time that evening. It was a fitting climax to a dizzying religious romance, as my bride and I were fully reunited through Christ and his Bride.

Kimberly:

One week after Hannah's baptism we moved to Joliet, Illinois. It was a very busy time for us, adjusting to the move into the first home we had ever owned, adjusting to our new baby and beginning the adventure of home-schooling for the first time. Scott was teaching full time at the College of Saint Francis in the theology department and loving it. Life was so full!

This was really "*spring*" thaw for me after the winter. My heart wanted to study, especially baptism. Scott found time to watch the children so that I could go study. Rather than seeing my seminary days as a waste, I realized I had gained tools with which I could pore over the Scriptures in serious study. I was in for a delightful surprise as I studied Catholic biblical scholars—for some reason I had thought Catholics mostly quoted papal documents. I came to appreciate that Hannah had become a child of God through baptism, being born again by water and the Spirit. As I studied baptism, it connected with what I had already done on justification. As with Scott, my study in seminary had led me to reject as unscriptural the Protestant teaching of justification by faith alone. Infant baptism highlighted justification by grace alone. I was amazed how beautiful the Scripture studies by Catholics were in regard to justification and baptism.

I had not been back to Mass since the Easter Vigil when Scott came into the Church, two years before. When I attended the Ash Wednesday service in a little chapel, I was amazed how deeply the liturgy touched me. The call to repentance was so clear, I wondered how several ex-Catholic friends had missed it when they said they had never been called to the gospel in the Catholic Church.

As soon as Scott became Catholic, it seemed that our boys (aged two and three at the time) began talking about being priests. I could not believe my ears! It really cut me to the quick at the time. Yet in Joliet I had met a number of wonderful, faith-filled priests. And I found my heart changing direction regarding God's call in the lives of our sons. When our son Gabriel, the three-year-old, said, "Mom, there aren't enough priests and nuns in the world. I want to be a priest and go all over the world making more priests and nuns", I found my heart pleased with his desire. This kind of change could come only from the Lord.

I began to phrase questions differently when I went to prayer. I started to ask the Lord to give me his heart and mind on the Eucharist and the other sacraments. Instead of pain-filled cries resulting from Scott-versus-Kimberly confrontations over these issues, I began approaching God, desiring his perspective, even if it was Roman Catholic.

There were still times of utter anguish—of feeling that I was being sucked into the void; that I was not thinking clearly enough, because if I was, I would see the faults of the Catholic Church. There were still times of weeping so deeply from the gut that I could barely breathe as the agony of the unknown pressed upon me.

But now there were also times of incredible grace when there were breakthroughs for me. I could not always figure out where my convictions ended and my obstinacy began. But God, in his mercy, was guiding.

Scott and I agreed that when Michael was seven, he would receive First Communion, and the children would become Catholic. I had to put that timetable out of my thoughts, though. I could not deal with the pressure of it. Instead, I tried to focus on the issues.

Scott encouraged me to take an opportunity to visit friends who were ministers in Virginia in the spring of

1988. I had a lot of questions I was hoping they could help me resolve.

It was a very fruitful trip, renewing friendships strained by Scott's conversion and having challenging conversations on theology. As I began to share with our friends why Scott said what he said, I became more convinced of the logic behind his arguments, though I did not necessarily want to be.

First, Jack and I went phrase by phrase through John 6:52–69, examining the Catholic position. Though I had read John through many times in my life, I had never been struck before by the force of Jesus' words as he says over and over that his body and blood are to be eaten (even chewed) and drunk to receive his life.

I said, "Jack, what do you do with that?"

"I think Jesus is teaching about faith, Kimberly."

This was the same analysis we had been given in the class we had taken together in seminary.

"Wait a minute. Are you basing that on the phrase 'the flesh is of no avail', in verse 63? Read the rest of the verse. 'It is the Spirit that gives life, the flesh is of no avail.' It's the Spirit that gives life. In other words, Jesus wasn't saying to the people, come on up and one of you can have a finger and one of you can have a toe. He was pointing to a time after his death, Resurrection and Ascension when the Spirit would give the disciples his glorified body so that his flesh would be life-giving for the world.

"Besides, Jack, why would it have offended the Jews so much if Jesus was only talking about faith and a symbolic sacrifice of his flesh and blood? They left disgusted, thinking he was talking about cannibalism. Why did Jesus allow most of his disciples to leave under a basic misunderstanding and never clarify for even his closest disciples that he was only talking about faith in a mere symbol of his eventual sacrifice? At least for his closest disciples, he cleared up misunderstandings of teachings in other passages of Scripture."

Jack did not see the difficulties I was seeing with a Protestant understanding of this passage, but I was feeling the force of Catholic arguments for the first time. This discussion shed light for me on a different problem I had had with transubstantiation: How could Jesus, in his humanity, give his actual body and blood to his disciples at the Last Supper? And if he didn't do it there, then why should we say it is more than symbol in our imitation of his act?

I knew Catholics said it was a miracle, but that seemed too facile an explanation until I tied it into the earlier teaching in John 6 of the miracle of the loaves and fishes. This multiplication of food was to point the way to the miraculous multiplication of the body and blood of Jesus for the life of the world. And though in his humanity alone, Jesus could not have separated his body and blood in the Upper Room to offer it to the disciples, he never was only human. Since Jesus was fully divine as well as fully human, he could have sat there in his body and blood and at the same time turned the bread and wine into his body and blood.

Next I visited another pastor friend, Bill, and his wife, Lisanne. After some conversation, Bill asked, "What's going to happen to your children?"

"Our children will be raised Catholic eventually. I really have no other option."

"You do have another option", Bill assured me. "You could take the children with you in a divorce, because he's abandoned the faith and embraced heresy."

"That's not a possibility, Bill, because I know that Scott has acted with too much integrity as a Christian simply to write him off spiritually, taking away the children."

Bill and Lisanne asked lots of questions and gave me a real chance to share my heart, unlike most Protestant friends we had. Later in the conversation, I said, "Look, I'm not a relativist and neither are you. If I join the Catholic Church—and I don't want to—but if I become convinced it's true, I want to take y'all in with me!"

(A few months later Bill called Scott to apologize for giving me the advice to divorce him and said my explanations of Scott's beliefs had been so convincing he was beginning to study the Catholic Church in earnest. Lisanne became my long-distance study partner. She and I were in similar situations: both needing to study these things and having mixed emotions about doing it. We would study a topic or book and then have one- to three-hour conversations about twice a month. Months after my conversion, both Bill and Lisanne came into the Church amidst many sufferings related to excommunication from their church and denomination.)

I came home from the trip with mixed emotions. More pieces had fallen into the Catholic puzzle, and yet I could tell that some of my Protestant friendships might become quite tenuous if I continued my search. There were still times of depression and isolation. And I felt mistrusted by some new Catholic friends.

I was not sure Catholics even believed what I was studying that Catholics supposedly believed. When we would go to Mass, people would come in and leave their coats on, looking like they were ready to bolt as soon as they received the Host. (I would never go to dinner at someone's home and leave my coat on!) For an evangelical Protestant used to fellowship and friendly conversation after the service, it was a shock to discover that most people did not intend to stay and greet one another.

I watched as people would receive and go right on out the door—I guess they wanted to be the first out of the parking lot. Can you imagine going to dinner somewhere and not even thanking the host who had provided the meal? And yet, supposedly, these people were receiving the Lord of the universe, the God-man who had died to save them! And they had no time to give him thanks for this incredible gift! Scott called this the Judas Shuffle— receive and leave.

One evening, we had an opportunity to be at a Mass where there was a eucharistic procession at the end. I had never seen this before. As I watched row after row of grown men and women kneel and bow when the monstrance passed by, I thought, These people believe that that is the Lord, and not just bread and wine. If this is Jesus, that is the only appropriate response. If one should kneel before a king today, how much more before the King of Kings? the Lord of Lords? Is it safe not to kneel?

But, I continued to ruminate, what if it's not? If that is not Jesus in the monstrance, then what they are doing is gross idolatry. So, is it safe to kneel? This situation highlighted what Scott had said all along: the Catholic Church is not just another denomination—it is either true or diabolical.

Since I had to decide, because the monstrance was coming closer, I gave it a half-hearted, half-up and half-down motion. Once again I felt nudged by the Holy Spirit to continue to take my study seriously, because this was not as simple as picking my favorite denomination.

Though I was not ready to make a commitment to the Catholic Church, I was already being cut off by some new fundamentalist friends because they felt I was becoming too Catholic. It was as if they could not see that we both sat on the Father's lap—as if they were trying to shove me off, saying, "You don't have a right to be here! You're going to become Roman Catholic!"

Yet I still had major obstacles to conversion, especially Mary. Scott understood that—he'd been there, too, at one time. When Scott heard that Dr. Mark Miravalle was coming to give a presentation on Mary at our college, he invited me to the lecture. I thought it would be helpful to hear a presentation, getting me out of the head-to-head combat in which Scott and I usually engaged.

I did not like everything I heard; I had a lot of questions. But I was not as defensive as usual. I listened as Dr. Miravalle clarified what the Catholic Church taught about Mary. First, she was not a goddess—she was worthy of honor and veneration but not worthy of worship, which is to be given to God alone. Second, Mary was a creature uniquely fashioned by her Son as no other mother has ever been or will be. Third, Mary rejoiced in God her Savior, as she stated in the Magnificat, because Jesus saved her from sin from the moment of conception. In other words, her sinlessness was a gift of grace, saving her before she sinned. (Certainly God had saved many of us from wild profligacy before we got into it; perhaps he saved Mary even earlier. I granted that it was possible.)

Fourth, Mary's title as Queen of Heaven did not come from being married to God—as I had thought—but was based on the honor of being the Queen Mother of Jesus, the King of Kings and the Son of David. In the Old Testament, King Solomon, the son of David, elevated his mother, Bathsheba, to a throne at his right hand, paying her homage in his court as the queen mother. And in the New Testament, Jesus elevated his mother, the Blessed Virgin Mary, to a throne at his right hand in heaven, bidding us to pay her homage as the Queen Mother of heaven.

Fifth, Mary's mission was to point beyond herself to her Son, saying, "Do whatever he says." At this point I realized that certain examples of Marian piety that focused on Mary to the point of neglecting Jesus perhaps were not faithful to Catholic teaching on her. Perhaps these dear souls did not even realize it, but they were offending the Blessed Virgin even in their attempts to honor her, if they were neglecting her primary mission to bring us to her Son.

When Scott and I got home that night, we had a good talk about Dr. Miravalle's points. He added a description of Mary as God's masterpiece that I found helpful.

"Mary is God's masterpiece. Have you ever walked into a museum where an artist was displaying his work? Can you imagine his being offended if you were viewing what he considered to be his masterpiece? Would he resent your looking at that instead of at him? 'Hey, you should be looking at me!' Rather, the artist would receive honor because of the attention you were giving his work. And Mary is God's work, from beginning to end."

Scott continued, "And if someone praises one of our children to you, do you interrupt with, 'Let's give credit where credit is due?' No, you know you are being honored when our child is being honored. Likewise, God receives glory and honor when his children are honored."

I took these thoughts to prayer that night and for the first time asked God what he thought about Mary. The phrases that came to my heart were these: "She's my beloved daughter", "my faithful child", "my beautiful vessel", and "my ark of the covenant bearing Jesus to the world".

I could not figure out why it was that it seemed to be that Catholics worshiped Mary, even though I knew worship of Mary was clearly condemned by the Church. Then I got an insight: Protestants defined worship as songs, prayers and a sermon. So when Catholics sang songs to Mary, petitioned Mary in prayer and preached about her, Protestants concluded she was being worshiped. But Catholics defined worship as the sacrifice of the Body and Blood of Jesus, and Catholics would never have offered a sacrifice of Mary nor to Mary on the altar. This was helpful food for thought.

Many major theological questions were resolved, but there was a wall, an emotional block, that took a supernatural gift of faith even to want to look over, let alone climb over. In November 1988, I wrote, "Where there is death, God can bring resurrection; yet the thing has to be completely dead to be raised. Am I dead yet? Am I fully yielded to you, Lord, to die to self and to live in you? It is very difficult to dodge depression and despair. As I muddle in the middle, I praise you, Lord; for you know the end from the beginning."

One day I was having a particularly difficult day with the children when a friend called. I shared that it was a tough day, and he said, "Why don't you think about Mary as a wonderful mother that you can go to and ask for help?"

I said, "Let's be honest. First, you're telling me that I'm dealing with a woman who never sinned. Second, you're telling me this woman had only one child, and he was perfect. Just think about it: something goes wrong at the dinner table, and everyone looks at Saint Joseph—it had to be his fault!

"I don't even believe in going to the saints for prayer. But if I did, I'd go to Joseph. I can't even relate to Mary!"

(Later on I shared this story with a friend who was troubled about the fact that I couldn't relate to Mary. After thinking about it awhile, she said, "Kimberly, what you said is true—she was perfect, and she had only one, perfect child—but if she's really the mother of all believers, just think how many difficult children she's had!")

It was at this time that God, in his mercy, allowed us special suffering: we miscarried two babies in 1989, one in January (Raphael) and one in December (Noel Francis). I say *in his mercy* because he has a tremendous way of using pain and suffering to strip a lot of nonessentials away and to draw us closer to him. As Mother Teresa says, our sufferings are God's gentle caresses, beckoning us to come back to him, to admit we are not in control of our lives, but he is in control and can be trusted with our lives completely. I realized much more deeply the truths I had already embraced about contraception relative to God's gifts of new life and began to understand in a personal way the redemptive nature of our suffering.

Heaven became a much fuller reality; for up until then, I had thought of heaven as only Jesus and me. I had been taught that to think of being with anyone else in heaven was in some way to detract from the glory and wonder of being with Jesus. But with each miscarriage a part of me had died. I longed to be with and hold those children and know those precious souls. The joy of being reunited

with those you love—parents, siblings and children—
who, with you, love the Lord is a joy that demonstrates
the glory of God, refracting the light of his glory rather
than detracting from his glory.

Heaven is described as a great celebration, the marriage
feast of the Lamb! Surely as love is perfected, it is not
annihilated but comes to its fullest flowering in the presence of our God.

After tubal pregnancy surgery on January 22, 1989, I
lay in my hospital room filled with emptiness. I had such
a sense of loneliness—from the loss of this life within and
from intense physical pain from the C-section cut I had
been given (without the typical consolation of a little one
to hold). Scott had gone home to be with our three other
children, who were not permitted to visit me in the hospital during my four-day recovery. And, to make matters
worse, the doctor had stuck me in a maternity ward,
where I could hear babies and their mothers throughout
the days of my stay.

As I poured out my heart to the Lord, picturing my
baby separated from me but in his arms, he brought to
mind Scriptures I had memorized long ago from
Hebrews 11 and 12. (Please note how important it was
that I had memorized these Scriptures so that God could
bring them to my heart in a time of crisis when I had no
access to his Word. Catholics can and must memorize
Scripture—Protestants have no special gene that makes it
easier for them to do it!)

Hebrews 11 is that great faith chapter listing wonderful
saints who risked so much, including their lives, for God.
At the beginning of chapter 12, it says, "Therefore, since
we are surrounded by so great a cloud of witnesses, let us
lay aside every sin and weight that so easily besets us and

let us run with perseverance the race set before us, keeping our eyes fixed on Jesus, the pioneer and perfecter of our faith."

I thought, in my Protestant understanding, that the communion of saints I affirmed in the Creed meant that the saints in heaven have communion among themselves and the saints on earth have communion among themselves but that the contact between heaven and earth is only between each one of us and the Lord. After all, the Old Testament clearly condemned necromancy—contacting the dead to find out the future.

But Hebrews 12 seemed to say that we were surrounded (present tense) in our race down here by all the brothers and sisters who had gone before us. In other words—I was not alone in my hospital room. I knew Jesus was there, but so were many other brothers and sisters who had gone before me. It was as if we were in an Olympic stadium and the people in the stands were former medalists in the race in which I was now competing—they knew what it took to win, and they were surrounding me and cheering me on.

In that cloud of witnesses present right there in my hospital room, there would have been saints who had lost children much older than my baby, whose spouses had died (not simply gone home to care for other children), whose experience with loneliness was worse than any I had experienced and whose physical condition had been worse than mine. Yet they were not there in judgment over me, clucking their tongues at my miserable failure to overcome sadness and loneliness. Rather, they were there to minister to me for the Lord in their compassion and prayers for me as I lay there in so much pain and sorrow.

If the prayers of a righteous man are very powerful, as James 5:16 says, how much more those who are perfected? If I could ask my mother on earth to pray for me and know that God would hear her petitions, why couldn't I ask the Mother of Jesus to pray for me? This was not the same as necromancy—these souls were the living, not the dead. And I was not asking them to foretell the future; I was asking them to intercede on my behalf just as I asked my brothers and sisters in Christ here on earth to intercede for me. I was not approaching them instead of Jesus but rather going with them to Jesus, just as I did on earth.

This prayer for intercession did not detract from the glory of God; it demonstrated his glory, because we were living faithfully as brothers and sisters in him. More Scriptures were falling into place, and I began to rejoice in the rich doctrine of the communion of saints—these people really were my older siblings in the Lord!

Up to this point, crucifixes had always bothered me. Yet as I lay on hospital beds (I had three hospitalizations related to one miscarriage alone), I looked at the crucifix, and I prayed, "Jesus, the very fact that you were on that Cross makes sense out of my suffering, because I can offer it to you. And yet the suffering I have undergone isn't anything compared with the suffering that you've undergone." His suffering put my suffering in perspective. I was so grateful for that. These hospitalizations were God's tool to draw me closer to him than ever before.

The next time we were at Mass as a family, I had such a sense that our whole family was united. Scripture taught that those in heaven participate in the same liturgy as those on earth. So in the presence of the Lord our family was one.

I spoke with my younger sister, who had had five miscarriages, about how she faced the possibility of the pain of miscarriage again and again. Kari described those precious children she and her husband had lost as treasure stored in heaven. I realized that, like her, Scott and I had treasures in heaven with these two precious souls. The Lord was allowing us to have special prayer warriors for our family.

Then our daughter, Hannah (aged one and a half), was in the hospital at Easter with dehydration. It was one thing for me to be in the hospital with my own suffering and another to be at my daughter's bedside with her suffering day and night. At the time she was hospitalized, she had a very high fever, and on the fifth day it spiked to 105.2 degrees.

The nurses came racing in and began putting ice-cold cloths on her body to break the fever quickly. I had been sleeping in her room, so I jumped up to help. Thankfully, since I was not a nurse, I had no idea how serious the situation was.

As soon as her hot little body heated up the towel, we took it off and put on another cold one. It was imperative that we get her fever down. Hannah was lying there with one arm bound by an IV tube and the other stretched toward me as far as she could reach, her whole body shaking so hard. She was screaming, "Mommy! Mommy!"

Hannah could not understand what I was doing. I was supposed to protect her from harm, yet here I was helping to put the cloths on her that were causing her much pain and discomfort. I could not explain it to her, but I knew I was doing the most loving thing for her.

In the midst of this, I felt the Lord put his hand on my shoulder and say, "Kimberly, do you see what a good

parent you are? You love your daughter, so you are causing her pain to heal her. Do you see how much I have
loved you, my daughter? I have caused you pain to heal
you, to draw you to myself." Though the nurses focused
on assisting Hannah, there was a deeper healing going on
inside of me at that moment, and I wept for both of us.

At this point in my life, I realized I might be facing a
new grief: If I decided no longer to be the only Protestant in my immediate family, I was going to have a new
separation as the only Catholic in my extended family.
How could I choose to be separated from my family,
within which I had been raised and had shared tremendous spiritual bonds? How could it be that the very persons who brought me to the table of the Lord would no
longer be able to partake with me? These were new
questions and sorrows.

Conversations with my parents and siblings became
more difficult over passages of Scripture—the very Scriptures my parents had taught me to know and love. It was
also very difficult for my siblings to see the pain I was
causing our parents. And I know my parents revealed rel-
atively little of that pain to my siblings in order to keep
my relationships with them intact. (They are noble souls,
who bore much of their agony together before the Lord.)

At that time I wrote, "The vibrancy of Mom and
Dad's faith and their own willingness to change as they
grow are a clear witness to me to follow Christ in his
Word where I am convicted he is leading. I cannot spare
them the grief they have and will know as I walk this
path. I have not sought this path, but God in his grace
and mercy has set me upon it."

In Chicago, Scott and I discovered a special group at
this time called the Society of Saint James. We made a

number of new friends who were like-minded people (unlike our Protestant friends who did not want to hear anything, or our Catholic friends who could not imagine what was keeping me from committing myself to the Catholic Church). These were people on pilgrimage, in transition, asking many of the questions I was asking. It was a delight to meet people who valued the agonizing efforts it was taking us to reach unity spiritually and who rejoiced in the discoveries I was making.

I took the Rite of Christian Initiation of Adults (RCIA) class the next year at Saint Patrick's church to sort through issues in a more conventional way. So much of the Catholic Faith made sense, but much was still unclear. It reminded me of our initial weeks in our new home in Joliet: Scott was already busy teaching classes at the College of Saint Francis, and I had full-time care of our newborn daughter and our sons aged three and four. That did not leave a lot of time for unpacking boxes. When I would get discouraged about the slow progress in unpacking, I would go into our lovely dining room, shield my eyes so I could not see the boxes, and simply enjoy the beauty of the room. Once again I could believe that soon life would be normal. Could it be that way in the Catholic Church? It could be, if only I knew what was in the boxes. In other words, the beauty of the Church was speaking to my heart, but there were still too many unknowns to act as if everything had been un-packed.

One of the classes shed some light on a bothersome topic: statues and pictures of Jesus, Mary and the saints. I asked, "Why are those allowed and even encouraged, when one of the Ten Commandments condemns the making of graven images and bowing down before them?"

Father Memenas responded with a question. "Kimberly, do you have a place in your home for family photos?"

"Yes."

"Why? What do they do for you?"

"The pictures remind me of these wonderful people I love—our parents, siblings, children. . . ."

"Kimberly, do you love the photos themselves or the people they represent?"

"Of course, the latter."

"That's what the paintings and statues do—they remind us of these wonderful brothers and sisters who have gone before us. We love them and thank God for them.

"The critical question is not whether or not these images should exist, because the Old Testament records, soon after the Ten Commandments are listed, specific instructions for images that were to be made as part of the Holy of Holies—garden imagery and the cherubim over the mercy seat, for example. God even commanded Moses to make a bronze serpent on a pole, which the people were to look upon in order to be healed from a plague. Either God got his commands mixed up, or the point of the command is not to worship images (as the Jews did at Mount Sinai with the golden calf) rather than not to have them."

This discussion and others gave me much food for thought. One dilemma loomed: Now that I was being drawn toward the Church, what was I to do with all the angry, sad feelings I had harbored toward the Church? I had detested the Church at times, blaming it for the disunity of my marriage, hating it for the disruption of happy family life, railing at it for the lack of joy in my own relationship to God because of its meddling in my life. I had grieved over the loss of dreams. Yet now my "enemy" was becoming my friend, or so it seemed.

When I took this in prayer to the Lord, I really sensed God saying, "You've got to see me behind it. You've blamed Scott, and you've blamed the Catholic Church. But you've got to understand I'm the One behind it all. I can take your anger."

I felt like a little child when I went to bed that night, because I let God have it. I felt like a little kid sitting on her dad's lap, pummeling his chest and crying until falling asleep exhausted. I did not resolve it further.

In the morning, I received a call from a friend of mine, Bill Stehltemeyer from EWTN. He said, "Kimberly?"

I said, "Hello!"

"I was having devotions this morning, and the Lord told me to call you and say, 'Kimberly, I love you.' That's all."

I did not connect that with the night before until my mother said the same thing later that day—and my Mom does not usually say such things as the Lord put something specific on her heart for me. All of a sudden I realized that what he was saying was, "Kimberly, I took that anger. I absorbed it. I still love you. You see, I'm really for you, I'm behind you, I'm guiding you." I had a deep sense of peace.

Besides taking the RCIA, I also helped out with Michael's CCD class, as much to find out what those Catholics were going to teach him as to offer service to the parish. Every class, we went over the Our Father, the Glory Be and the Hail Mary. I prayed the Our Father and the Glory Be, but I would not say the Hail Mary. I learned it, but I would not practice it.

By the time we got to first confession, I believed it was a sacrament. I was particularly glad for one little girl—if anyone needed first confession, it was she. When she came back from seeing the priest, she seemed about to cry.

"Is something wrong?" I asked.

"Father said to say the Hail Mary", she replied.

"Well, you better go ahead and say it", I responded.

"I don't remember it."

Now I was faced with another dilemma. I was not saying the Hail Mary yet because I was not sure it did not offend God; but I knew she had to say her penance for the sacrament to be valid. I swallowed hard and said, "Repeat after me: Hail, Mary."

"Hail, Mary."

"Full of grace . . ."

We went through the whole thing, and when we finished, she looked up at me with her big eyes and said, "Two times."

I knew she had really needed that sacrament! So I took another big breath and started saying it again. Many people can't recall when they first said the Hail Mary, but I have quite a vivid memory of my first time!

A friend, Dave, from Milwaukee called one night to see if he could talk to me about what still blocked my coming into the Church. I told him the issue was still whether or not Mary was my spiritual mother. He said, "What do you think about Revelation 12?"

"I don't know. I don't think I've ever read that. Let me get my Bible."

When I came back to the phone with my Bible, Dave explained, "The chapter is about four main characters who are in battle. Even if they are symbolic for other groups of people, they are specific people, too. The woman with the man-child is Mary with Jesus.

"Look at verse 17, 'Then the dragon was angry with the woman and went off to make war on the rest of *her* offspring, on those who keep the commandments of God and bear testimony to Jesus. . . .' "

I was stunned. How had I missed that passage in my study on Mary? I had to admit, "I guess that means that if I bear testimony to Jesus and keep his commandments, then spiritually she is my mother. What do you know! Mary's a warrior maiden who does battle through her motherhood." I could relate to that.

This passage helped clarify why, at the foot of the Cross, when he was in utter agony, Saint John 19:26–27 records, "When Jesus saw his mother and the disciple whom he loved standing near, he said to his mother, 'Woman, behold, your son!' Then he said to the disciple, 'Behold, your mother!' And from that hour the disciple took her to his own home." With this passage as the basis, the Catholic Church taught that Jesus' gift of Mary to the "beloved disciple" was a prefigurement of his giving her to each of his beloved disciples.

I was a beloved disciple. Did I, like John, need to receive her into my home as my mother, too? Instead of seeing Mary as a tremendous obstacle to me, I was beginning to see her as a precious gift from the Lord—one who loved me, cared for me and prayed for me with a mother's heart. She was no longer just a doctrine to understand; she was a person to embrace with my whole heart!

I was still undecided about becoming a Catholic by that Easter. On Ash Wednesday I dropped off our children at my sister's home so I could look for housing for us in Steubenville. (Scott had just received a contract from Franciscan University of Steubenville.) Since it was Ash Wednesday, I was asking God what I should give up for Lent: chocolate, desserts . . . major sacrifices on my part.

And I really sensed the Lord say, "Kimberly, why don't you give up?"

"What? Give up what?"

He said, "Why don't you give up yourself? You know enough to trust me and to trust my work in the Church. Your heart attitude has changed from saying, 'I don't believe it—prove it!' to saying, 'Lord, I don't understand it. Teach me.' Why don't you come to the table? Why don't you give up *you* this Lent?"

I really sensed the Lord was the One calling me into the Catholic Church. I spent the rest of the next four hours praying and praising him, having a deep peace that this was it. Was Scott in for a surprise!

The next night, after listening to descriptions of the houses I had seen, he said, "By the way, I'm at this conference on apologetics out here in California and everyone's asking where you are in relation to the Church." He was trying so hard to sound casual about it. He had learned the difference between his sharing and the Holy Spirit's convicting. "I'm not pressuring you at all. If it's not this Easter, that's no problem. But do you have any idea where you are in the process?"

I could hardly wait to tell him. "It's going to be this Easter, Scott. The Lord spoke to my heart in the van and said it's going to be this Easter. Scott? Scott, are you there?"

It took him a minute to regain his composure. "Praise the Lord!" For the first time Scott was able to dream about what was possible if we were a united Catholic family. There was such joy! There was such freedom!

It was time. Time to be reunited under Scott's spiritual leadership. Time to have a common vision within the Church for ministry we could have as a couple. Time for me to decide that the answers I did not have I could find in the Church Jesus himself had founded and preserved from error. Time for me to let go of the struggle and to be thankful to God for what he had revealed to me.

Though I had believed in transubstantiation for more than a year, I had had no yearning to receive. But now a hunger for the Eucharist became the last thought of the day and the first thought of the morning. I had received Jesus as Savior and Lord by faith when I was a teenager, but now I longed to receive his Body and Blood. For not only had Jesus humbled himself on our behalf in taking on human flesh to be our perfect sacrifice; he had even condescended lower—to offer us that same flesh to be the life and food of our souls! All this so that we could have him within us—not only in our hearts but in our physical bodies as well, making us living tabernacles. I felt that my heart would burst with so much joy!

Sharing the news was not easy. There were some people who rejoiced so much that it was very humbling, to say the least. ("You don't know how many Rosaries I've said for you to convert!") There were Protestant friends who were incredulous that after four years I had folded. ("That's tragic!") For my family, there was a lot of sadness; they did not reject me because of my decision, but their hearts hurt for love of me and concern over what ramifications this decision could have in our larger family.

When I called my parents to let them know I had

decided to be received into the Catholic Church that Easter, Dad did not discourage or encourage me. He just asked me, "Kimberly, Jesus is the one to whom you are accountable. When you put Jesus in front of you, what can you say to him in good conscience?"

And I replied, "Dad, I would say with my whole heart: Jesus, I have loved you at great cost, and I have been obedient to all that I have understood, following you right into the Catholic Church."

"Kimberly, if that's what you would say, then that's what you must do."

The weeks of Lent were filled with special graces for Scott and me. My concerns about going to confession melted—I could not wait to get there.

One day a couple of weeks before Easter, Scott said, "Why don't you pray the Rosary?"

In my typically docile manner I said, "I'm becoming Catholic, Honey. Don't push it."

He responded, "Well, it was just a suggestion."

The next week Scott was visiting EWTN when Bill Stehtlemeyer said, "By the way, the Holy Spirit told me that I'm supposed to mail my Rosary to your wife."

Thinking of our recent conversation, Scott said, "I don't know if I would do that."

Bill was not put off. "The Holy Father gave this Rosary to me, and I never thought I'd part with it. But the Holy Spirit told me to give it to Kimberly, so I'm going to mail it to your wife."

Scott recounted this story to me and gave me a book on the scriptural Rosary, leaving it all in my hands. When the Rosary arrived, I looked at it and I thought, what a treasure for anyone who is Catholic. I really can't just let this sit in my drawer. And yet, dare I use it?

I was concerned that the Rosary was an example of vain repetition that had been clearly condemned by Jesus. However, an introduction to the Rosary by a nun helped give me a new perspective. She urged believers to see themselves, not as great, big adult Christians, but as little children before the Lord. For example, she reminded the reader that when our own young children say, "I love you, Mommy" over and over in a day, we never turn to them and say, "Honey, that's just vain repetition!" Likewise, we as young children were saying "I love you, Mommy, pray for me" to Mary through the Rosary. Though repetitious, it became vain only if we said the words without meaning them.

The first three days I prayed a decade of the Rosary, saying, "Lord, I hope this is not going to offend you." After a few days I really felt the Lord was giving his approval and ministering to me through it. It became a regular part of my life. Then I decided to tell Scott that I was praying with the Rosary. This was another in a series of times when, through tears and hugs, I was humbled to admit to Scott he had been right about various things. And I read what I had just written in my prayer journal:

> Break apart my cold heart in the spring thaw of your Spirit. I want to get out of the way and let you work through me. Please forgive me for the years I have rejected Scott's spiritual leadership and replace my heart of stone with a heart of flesh—your eucharistic flesh. Thank you for the opportunity to have my filthy sins taken away by your powerful graces in the sacrament of confession and penance, allowing me to participate in repairing the damage I have done to the Body of Christ.

I've thoroughly enjoyed the Bridegroom and his Father, and I'm anticipating the wedding feast to come, but Jesus wants me also to know his Bride, the Church, and to realize more fully with whom I will be celebrating. What groom would want me simply to come to the feast and stare at him? He wants me to know his bride and to cherish her, too. The Church has been an abstraction until now for me, only spiritual and not tangible. But now she's becoming more than uplifting sermons and challenging services; she's becoming personal. More than a collection of doctrines that are truer and richer than what I've had before, the Church is becoming a living, breathing entity filled with faulty persons, like myself, who are sick and needing a physician, all the while covered with the tremendous glory of God.

I'd committed to giving up me for Lent and yet, as is always true with God, what have I given up but what I didn't want to hold onto. Your love has broken through, O God. Yes, Scott was right. Why were you doing this to me? To demonstrate your love for me.

In Grove City I remember the day I began to feel I didn't know who you were: the God of the Protestants or of the Catholics. Were you just rooting for Scott and angry at me? I wondered. But I wouldn't budge. I would not read or study or even pray—it was too painful. I didn't want to die—to dreams, to visions, to my M.A., to my understanding of the truth. I had it down pat. To redefine theological terms or risk losing friendships or hurting my family—it just couldn't be. It was a nightmare from which I was sure I would awaken.

But now, Lord, I can sense your love for me throughout. You don't just love me now that I've come to this truth. You've loved me every step of the way—for who I was, not just for what I would become.

Please teach me all over again. I want to be pliable. I've been broken. Pour on the oil of your joy to take the broken pieces of clay and make them moldable. My heart sings anew the goodness of the Lord.

The crosses you have given me through Scott and from myself these last seven years are gifts. Suffering is having its way.

During a prayer time the week before Easter, I was amazed by how much the monstrance seemed to symbolize the Catholic Church. Like many Protestants, I had been concerned that Mary, the saints and the sacraments were roadblocks between believers and God so that, to get to God, one would have to go around them. They seemed to complicate life with God unnecessarily—like accretions on the sides of sunken treasures, they had to be discarded to get to what was important.

But now I could see that the opposite was true. Catholicism was not a distant religion, but a presence-oriented one. Catholics were the ones who had Jesus physically present in churches and saw themselves as living tabernacles after receiving the Eucharist. And because Jesus is the Eucharist, keeping him in the center allows all of the rich doctrines of the Church to emanate from him, just as the beautiful gold rays stream forth from the Host in the monstrance.

My Easter Vigil was to hold a joy mixed with sorrow similar to Scott's. My parents had decided to attend the Mass, since I was making a major, life-changing decision they believed they should witness. I was glad they had come, because it seemed to me that I should feel their pain at the separation I was causing, even while I was experiencing the joy of being received into the Church.

They came in love to be with us. We went out to dinner the night before, and I had a wonderful chance to share from my heart why I was becoming Catholic. I wanted them to know this was my decision, and it had been hard won through much prayer and study. In fact, I said that if Scott were to die the Monday after Easter, I would not consider dating a Protestant again because my faith had come at too dear a price.

I also wanted to tell them that I was not the primary cause of their pain but that the Lord was the One behind it all. For me, it had been so much easier to blame Scott for causing me pain or the Catholic Church for intruding into my life rather than to see the Lord's hand at work. But now I could see that God in his mercy had been meddling in my life because he loved me that much.

Easter Vigil morning Barb, a dear friend, brought three Easter lilies from a group of which our family had become a part. This group, Catholic Families and Friends, were planning a special party that night to celebrate with us. They wanted the house to be filled all day with a fragrance of joy. Next my sponsors, Dr. and Mrs. Al Szews, came from Milwaukee with special gifts. In preparation for the service, my parents prayed with me at home, and then my sponsors prayed with me at the church.

Following first confession, I prayed alone to prepare my heart for the Vigil Mass. I scrawled a note to Scott, "Dearest Scott, I am *so* thankful for you and for your forging this path for us. I love you. K." I didn't know how to express the abundant gratitude I felt in my heart for Scott's faithfulness to God.

In the pew behind me sat Scott, who wept with joy to see me come into the fullness of the Faith and receive the

Lord in the Eucharist with him, and my parents, who wept with sorrow to see me join myself to a Church they would never have chosen for me, which now separated us at the table of the Lord. I thought I could hardly bear the joy or the pain at the giving of the sign of peace.

Shortly after the service, the celebration began. My parents slipped away after a brief stay. The joy expressed for me was overwhelming. Easter Sunday, after the glorious morning Mass, our family went to Milwaukee, where we celebrated our becoming a Catholic family with dear friends in the Wolfe's home (Scott's sponsors). What indescribable joy! In my spiritual walk, "*summer*" had arrived.

Easter Vigil, 1990. The night Kimberly was received into the Church. Here with Scott and Fr. Memenas, St. Patrick's Church, Joliet, Illinois.

9

Catholic Family Life

Scott:

When evangelical Protestants convert to the Catholic
Church, they often enter into a kind of "ecclesiastical
culture shock". They leave robust congregational singing,
practical biblical preaching, a conservative pro-family
political voice in the pulpit and a vital sense of community, with various prayer meetings, fellowships and Bible
studies to choose from each week. In contrast, the average Catholic parish usually finds itself lacking in these
areas. While these converts typically feel that they have
"come home" by becoming Catholics, they do not
always *feel* "at home" in their new parish families. Kimberly and I both experienced this.

Places like Franciscan University of Steubenville prove
that this need not be so. What has impressed us the most
from our time in Steubenville is precisely the way it com-
bines the evangelical and the Catholic. I am talking about
the way in which the Catholic Faith unites what other
religions tend to separate: personal piety and liturgical rit-
ual; evangelistic outreach and social action; spiritual fer-
vor and intellectual rigor; academic freedom and dynamic
orthodoxy; enthusiastic worship and reverent contempla-
tion; powerful preaching and sacramental devotion;
Scripture and Tradition; body and soul; the individual
and the corporate.

Since Kimberly's conversion, we now share all of this as a family. We make an effort to attend daily Mass as a family at the University. With the Eucharist at the center of our lives, we are able to show our children how the Bible and the liturgy go together, the menu and the meal. Our kids see dozens of priests and hundreds of students who are living out the gospel in practical ways.

Teaching such students has proven to be one of the most rewarding experiences in my life. They have a passion to study Scripture, to learn theology and to ask hundreds of challenging questions. (I affectionately refer to the students as my "holy brainsuckers".) When class is over, they seek to apply the lessons they've learned in their work and relationships. I am convinced that God is raising up many of the future leaders of the Catholic Church here at the University.

Besides my work at the University, the Lord has given Kimberly and me numerous opportunities to minister across the country. With several hundred of my talks on audio and video cassettes, the message is reaching far beyond our limited range of travel. These tapes are now circulating in many countries. People have written and called from Canada, Mexico, England, Scotland, Holland, Poland, Lithuania, Belgium, Austria, Australia, New Zealand, Ghana, Japan, Indonesia, the Philippines and others; and to think that we feared we might never be able to minister together again!

All of this has been made possible through our partnership with Terry Barber and Saint Joseph Communications. Within one year's time, "The Tape", which recorded the talk that I gave to only thirty-five people back in 1989, had been purchased by more than thirty-five thousand. That number has climbed to the hundreds of thousands in the last few years. Besides the tape of my conversion story, Terry has released over two hundred of my tapes touching on a wide variety of subjects, explaining various aspects of the Catholic Faith.

My father was right after all—and he never let me forget it. He made sure that I knew how proud he was of his youngest son, the nonjeweler theologian.

After a long illness, he passed away in December 1991. It was one of the most difficult and yet most blessed experiences of my life. For many years he had been an agnostic, but through his suffering, he recovered a personal faith in Christ. During the last few weeks of his life, we were able to spend meaningful time together praying, reading Scripture and talking about his life and the Lord. I will never forget the privilege of holding his hand and closing his eyes when his heavenly Father called him to himself; nor will I ever stop thanking God for giving me an earthly father who made it so easy to love my heavenly Father.

One week later, my father-in-law, Dr. Jerry Kirk, called to invite me to accompany him to Rome the following month to meet with Pope John Paul II. Talk about the grace of God.

As the founder of R.A.A.P. (the Religious Alliance against Pornography), Jerry had been invited by members of the Roman hierarchy to conduct a three-day session in the Vatican with a group of a dozen major religious leaders from America. Cardinal Bernardin had organized the meetings in order to coordinate strategies with Vatican officials for combatting hardcore pornography worldwide. At the end of our deliberations, we were to have a private audience with the Holy Father to present our conclusions and to discuss them with him more closely.

So I went to Rome for the first time. In between meetings, I was able to visit Saint Peter's and a few other sacred sites—not as a tourist but as a pilgrim. It was over-whelming.

At the end of the three days, on a Thursday afternoon, we were taken through a labyrinth of corridors and ushered into a meeting room. As we sat there waiting for the Pope's arrival, I prayed intently. After he entered the room, the proceedings seemed to go by in a flash.

When they were over, Jerry had the privilege of intro-ducing each of us to the Pope. When it came my turn, I heard my father-in-law say to my spiritual father, "Your Holiness, I'd like to introduce you to Scott Hahn, a pro-fessor at Franciscan University of Steubenville."

I shook his hand, and that was it—on to the next reli-gious leader in line. Afterward, I stood there rejoicing and thanking God for the privilege of meeting my spiritual father in Christ, even if it was for just a few seconds. Still, I got to squeeze the hand of the Vicar of Christ, the suc-cessor to Peter—no small thrill for this former anti-Catholic.

One hour later the leaders were regathering in the Vat-ican chamber where we had been meeting all week. When I walked in, I heard gales of laughter coming from the direction of my mother-in-law, who was standing at a table staring at a photograph. I went to investigate. Standing next to her, I looked down and beheld a picture of her husband introducing her son-in-law to the Pope. "Can you believe it?! After all these years, your father-in-law gets to introduce *you* to the Pope." As she laughed more heartily, she hugged me warmly. What an awesome mother-in-law!

A few minutes later the phone rang in an office down

the hall. An older man came into the meeting room and asked, "Is Professor Scott Hahn here?"

I waved my hand to identify myself.

"A telephone call for you."

As I walked down the hall, I wondered, Who could it be? I picked up the phone and heard a heavily accented voice.

"Are you able to join His Holiness, Pope John Paul II, tomorrow morning at 7 A.M. for Mass in his private chapel?"

At first I thought it was a joke. Then I remembered a meeting earlier that week with Professor Rocco Buttiglione, who offered to use his influence with the Pope's private secretary to get me into the Pope's morning Mass.

"Yes, I can make it." But I was so nervous that I forgot to ask for the details.

Fortunately, Cardinal Cassidy, one of the Vatican officials in the meeting room, explained to me the procedure. I was to be at a certain gate by 6:30 A.M., where a Swiss guard would meet me.

The next morning, I got up after a futile struggle to sleep and took a taxi down to Saint Peter's. I got there more than an hour ahead of time. Pacing around Saint Peter's square, I prayed a Rosary and prepared myself for the privilege of a lifetime.

Sure enough, at the appointed time, someone came out to meet me. He led me down some stairs and through a series of corridors until I was standing amidst several bishops and priests who were vesting to concelebrate Mass with the Pope.

I stood there nervously, when suddenly the Pope's personal secretary stuck his head through the doorway and looked around the room. Finally, he spoke up. "Vare eese dee tay-ologee professor frum Stubbenveel Oooniver-sitee?"

I could barely piece together the question through his thick accent. Then it finally dawned that he was asking for me.

I waved my hand rather sheepishly and said, "Here I am."

He looked over and nodded his head. "Gute, I vill tell heem."

I had no idea what that was all about, but I got a kick out of all the foreign prelates looking my way and wondering, "Who is this guy and how does he rate?"

Moments later we were led down the hall and into a small private chapel. Upon entering, I noticed that Pope John Paul II was already there on his kneeler praying before the tabernacle. As I knelt a few feet away, I asked the Lord for a special grace to unite my heart with that of my spiritual father as he renewed the covenant and celebrated the sacrifice of Christ in the Mass.

What reverence and love were shown by the Pope at every point in the eucharistic liturgy. I recall how never before had I felt so vividly the reality of Christ's presence.

When Mass was over, the people were led out of the chapel while the Holy Father remained on his kneeler in thanksgiving. I was the last to leave. I couldn't resist the temptation. I stopped and knelt a few feet behind him and prayed—there alone with the Pope for maybe half a minute—until I heard footsteps scurrying down the hall to the chapel. Just as I suspected, they had taken a count and had found that someone was missing. I got up to go just as the Pope's personal secretary reentered the chapel. He guided me, firmly but gently, back into the room where the Pope would meet with us in a few minutes.

While waiting, I prayed and then rehearsed what I was to do—when suddenly the Pope walked into the room. What struck me almost immediately was how much more alert and energetic he appeared now, right after Mass, compared to the look of exhaustion I had seen on his face the day before during our private audience with him in the afternoon.

He seemed intensely interested in each one he spoke with as he walked around. He seemed to treat each person as though he were the only one in the room. He looked him right in the eyes and listened intently before speaking. Then my turn came.

He stepped up to greet me, and as I reached out with both arms, we embraced. I then handed him a beautifully packaged set of my tape series on "Answering Common Objections", along with an envelope that contained a personal letter and two checks as tokens of love and appreciation from the Barber and Hahn families.

He looked me right in the eyes and said, "God bless you. Are you the theology professor from Steubenville University?"

"Yes, I am."

"Please send my greetings and blessings to the community there in Steubenville."

"Holy Father, my own natural father just died last month, and now my heavenly Father has blessed me with the privilege of meeting you, my spiritual father." With that, we embraced a second time.

He stared intently and said, "I'm sorry to hear that your father died. God bless him. I'll pray for him."

My heart leapt as I immediately recalled a certain line of Scripture: "Whatever you bind on earth shall be bound in heaven . . ."

Then I briefly explained, in about a minute's time, all about my pilgrimage of faith as an anti-Catholic Presbyterian minister who had become a Catholic just six years before.

He listened carefully before giving me one more handshake, a blessing and a Rosary. As I left the presence of Pope John Paul II—the one anointed by my heavenly Father and eldest Brother to shepherd the covenant family of God on earth—I had a strong sense that God was saying, "Scott, the best is yet to come."

Kimberly:

Six weeks after I was received into the Church, our eldest son, Michael, made his First Communion. I had been a Catholic only a short time, and I felt that my heart was going to burst. I could not imagine what it felt like for those parents who as cradle Catholics had dreamt of the time they would get married, have a child and bring him to the table of the Lord for First Communion. (We have now had the opportunity to bring Gabriel to First Communion and are eagerly awaiting that special time with Hannah.)

The concerns on my heart each time have been these: first, I hoped the feast of the Passover Lamb from heaven was more important than the feast of the party afterward; and second, I hoped that the focus was on the presence of Jesus in the Eucharist rather than the presents the children would receive later.

Once, at the consecration of the Mass, Scott leaned over to me and said, "Can you imagine what the angels must think?"

His question led me to think about realities I'd not considered before. Certainly the angels are present for the liturgy, but they do not receive the Lord. They must peer down in wonder and awe at the incredible love our heavenly Father had for us in sending Jesus to earth to take on lowly human nature, to lay down that life in sacrifice for us and, finally, to feed us with that resurrected and glorified offering of his Body and Blood. What a glorious mystery!

Fasting for the hour beforehand has been a good experience, too, because it has been a small mortification (of which there are all too few in my life) to point to my need to hunger for souls.

Our move to Steubenville has been such a blessing. We have all made many wonderful friends at the University and in the community. There are more than forty families in our Heart of Mary Homeschool Support Group. And the college students have been a great reinforcement to our children of our own commitment to the Lord.

How is our life different? My heart is so full of the goodness of the Lord and so full of that joy of my salvation which for five years I really wanted to sense but could not. I guess I could summarize it in three phrases: unity restored, ministry renewed and family refreshed.

Our unity has been restored. We hold deep convictions in common once again—even deeper now after all we have been through. I love to sit under Scott's teaching once again. Instead of chafing during his Bible studies, I really enjoy them.

We come to the Lord's table together often at Franciscan University with a committed group of believers who love the Lord and want to share their love for God faithfully. The children had sensed our disunity, though we did not talk a great deal about our disagreements in front of them. Yet more than a mere sense of relief, the children have really shared our joy in being so deeply reunited.

We have had ministries renewed. Certain dreams died, but God has restored them superabundantly. In our home, we have had tremendous opportunities for hospitality, with over three hundred people for meals at our home yearly. In addition, having had a succession of college students move in with us has been a new adventure for us in extended household living. And our large living room accommodates crowds of between twenty and fifty for both Scott's and my weekly Bible studies.

Scott and I have begun speaking together on trips. We have had the privilege of meeting and sharing the Catholic Faith with so many wonderful, committed and growing Catholics all over our country. The tape ministry through Saint Joseph Communications has enabled our messages to go much farther than we could ever have traveled. And the ongoing ministry by phone and mail has challenged us to the limits of our time and energies! And to think these are all ministries that I thought were gone permanently, only to be restored in the Lord's time.

Our family has been so refreshed because there are new channels of grace open to us: regular confession and almost daily Eucharist. We have enjoyed learning about the liturgical calendar, observing the fasting (Advent, Lent, Fridays) and enjoying the feasting. (Besides birthdays and Christmas, we celebrate our saint days and our baptism anniversaries.)

I have had our first baby as a Catholic, knowing that every day as I received the Eucharist my baby was being

fed and nurtured by the Lord himself. After our miscarriages, I really did not have a certainty that I could bring
this baby to term, but I did know each day that I had the
opportunity to bring this little baby before the Lord and
receive the blessing of the priest. I also harnessed the
saints in heaven for the first time, asking for their intercession on my child's behalf. What joy it was to deliver
Jeremiah Thomas Walker on July 3, 1991, and have him
baptized in early September. And it was a tremendous joy
to us and a bridge to my family to have my father participate in Jeremiah's baptism.

We had not gone to daily Mass as a family until the
day I was received into the Church; now it's the goal of
our day. We have been blessed by many priests who stop
in Steubenville and assist at Mass. Amazed at the number
of priests, Hannah's regular question has become, "Is he
my father, too?"

We appreciated our evangelical tradition, where people sing and pray wholeheartedly. So, one of the elements
of worship our family has most appreciated at Franciscan
University is the way people participate. As Scott says, "If
the Eucharist doesn't make you want to sing, what
would?"

Though it is not always easy, it is always good to be
together at Mass. It is a good time for physical closeness
and for teaching the children about the Lord. Even
though there are times when it seems the grace received
has already been spent on the children before the end of
the closing hymn (due to discipline and distraction), it has
been better to have brought them into the presence of
Jesus than to have left them out. At the end of the Mass,
we have what we call our "holy huddle". We get real,
real close and offer a prayer of thanksgiving as a family.

I'm thankful for the unity of our family under Scott's spiritual leadership.

How sweet it is to be home in the Roman Catholic Church! And what a privilege it has been to reflect upon our lives and to share how our Lord has guided our steps to him and his Church. Surely, as the psalmist says, "He has caused his wonderful works to be remembered, the Lord is gracious and merciful" (Ps 111:4). May our Lord through his abundant mercy enable us all daily to give ourselves more fully to him.

The Hahn family. July, 1993.

Conclusion

Calling Catholics to Be Bible Christians (and Vice Versa)

We have now told our story. In closing, we want to give thanks to God for his grace and mercy. We also want briefly to share the challenge that God has put before us in his Word.

For our Catholic brothers and sisters, we want to encourage and challenge you to learn the Catholic Faith, which has been entrusted to you as a sacred heritage. For your own sake—and for others—study it so that you come to know *what* you believe and *why* you believe it. Pick up the Scriptures daily and read them. They are the inspired and inerrant Word of God written for you, as the Catholic Church has consistently taught throughout this century, especially in Vatican II. Believe what you read. Share it. Pray it. Memorize it. Soak in it, as in a warm tub! Learn it well so that you can live it more fully—and share it more joyfully. That is the way to make your faith infectious. We need more contagious Catholics!

Along with the Bible, pick up a copy of the *Catechism of the Catholic Church* and read through it—from cover to cover—at least once. It is indispensable for implementing the teachings of Vatican II. In fact, it is the "key to the Council". While you're at it, why not blow the dust off your copy of *The Documents of Vatican II* (you do have one, don't you?) and then spend a few weeks refreshing yourself with the real "spirit of the Council" drawn straight from the texts. Vatican II called for renewal, but the response to that call has been postponed. It will begin just as soon as average Catholics—like you and me—take these basic steps. It's really not that hard; any "Joe Six-pack-in-the-Pew" can do it!

The most important message of Vatican II—by far—is the "universal call to holiness". Basically it means that all Catholics—not just priests and religious—are called to be saints. That requires each of us to place the highest priority on prayer, *daily* prayer. As Americans, we often find ourselves "too busy" for developing and maintaining an interior life; but as Catholics, we know that it is absolutely essential—before all else. Make a "plan of life" for yourself so that prayer is on the schedule. That may sound easy, but it's really hard at times—though not nearly as hard as life apart from daily prayer.

The foundation for the Catholic's life must be the sacraments, especially the Eucharist. We can't make it on our own. Christ knew that; that's why he instituted the sacraments—to give us his own divine life and power. We must be careful not to receive the sacraments in a mindless manner. They are not magical or mechanical means to make us holy without personal faith and effort. The Catholic can't go through the eucharistic liturgy as a car goes through a carwash. It just doesn't work that way. Grace is not something that is *done* to us; rather, grace is the supernatural life of the Trinity planted deep within our souls so that God can make his home within us. This is the covenant that we are called to live as brothers and sisters in God's Catholic family. Christ is the food for our souls; let's stay off a starvation diet.

Catholics who cultivate prayer, study and a sacramental lifestyle must also become active apostles wherever they find themselves: at home, on the job, in the marketplace, but especially with family and friends. In recent years, the Catholic Church has lost literally millions of her members to fundamentalist and evangelical denominations and fellowships. This creates new and exciting opportunities, not only to win ex-Catholics back to the Church, but also to show non-Catholics the Catholic Faith for what it truly is: Bible-based and Christ-centered.

Let's face it, many of these non-Catholics put us to shame. With Bible in hand, plus lots of zeal, they do far more with less than many Catholics who have the fullness of Faith in the Church but who are famished and fast asleep. We share with them so much of the truth about Christ in Scripture; but what they lack is nothing less than the real and substantial presence of Christ in the Eucharist. To state it simply, they study the menu while we enjoy the Meal! And too often, we don't even know the ingredients, so we can't share the recipe. Is our Lord asking too much from Catholics to do more—much more—to help our separated brethren discover the Lord they love in the Blessed Sacrament? If we don't, who will?

We also want to share this challenge with our non-Catholic brothers and sisters in Christ. With love and respect, we testify to the covenant faithfulness of our God, who, down through the ages, has fathered one holy, catholic and apostolic Church family. Paul refers to this Church as "the household of God", which is "the pillar and foundation of truth" (1 Tim 3:15). This is another way of saying the family of God is divinely established and empowered to uphold revealed truth.

God fathers his family in one Church. After all, what do you call someone who fathers more than one family? He would have been called a scoundrel (or worse) where I came from; what a shame if you had to call him "Dad". A father is glorified by the oneness of his family; a man is disgraced when his children are separated. Real unity means a oneness of life that is experienced through oneness in belief and practice. All of this applies to the Church of God: one holy Father is able to preserve his one holy family—and this he has done in the Catholic Church.

It is this Church about which Christ spoke: "I will build *my* Church." She is not *your* Church, nor is she *mine*; she is Christ's. He is the builder; we are only the tools. Making much of the Church, then, is not to belittle our Lord. The Church is his handiwork. To acknowledge the greatness of the Church—her divine authority and infallible witness—is nothing less than magnifying the redemptive work of Christ. Conversely, to reject the authority and to spurn the witness of the Church—even when done with a misguided zeal for Christ's exclusive honor—is to defy him and the fullness of his grace and truth. Saul learned this lesson the hard way.

The Church is also called the Mystical Body of Christ; the Holy Spirit is her Soul. A body without a soul is a corpse; a soul without a body is a ghost. The Church of Christ is neither. But she can hardly be called a body if she lacks visible unity. In that case, Paul would not have called her Christ's Body but simply his Soul. But the soul is meant to animate the body, not to float around without it. When the soul does its job, all of the parts and members of the body are alive and healthy. Within the Church, these parts and members are called "saints".

Saints radiate the life of the Holy Spirit in the Body of Christ. This is the purpose of the Holy Spirit, then, to keep the visible Body of Christ alive in truth and holiness. He's been doing that for nearly two thousand years; it's called the Catholic Church. That these elements are so closely connected by the Apostles' Creed—"I believe in the Holy Spirit, the holy catholic Church, the communion of saints"—is no accident.

At the heart of this Catholic vision lies the Trinity. God is an eternal Family of three Divine Persons: the Father, the Son and the Holy Spirit. The covenant is what enables us to participate in his own divine life. For us that life means nothing less than our family share—as children of God—in the interpersonal communion of the Trinity. This is what Catholics mean by grace, *sanctifying* grace. This lofty understanding of grace is the basis for each and every distinctive Catholic belief. Whether it's Mary, the Pope, the bishops, the saints or the sacraments—it is all made possible by God's living and active grace. Divine grace is how God takes our fallen nature far beyond itself. (The key word here is "beyond"—not "against"—since grace does not destroy nature; rather, grace builds upon nature: to *heal* it, to *perfect* it and to *elevate* it so as to share God's life.) To call the Catholic Church the "family of God", then, is not a metaphorical statement; it is a metaphysical assertion. Indeed, it is the mystery of our Faith.

It is true, Jesus Christ wants to have a personal relationship with each of us as our Savior and Lord. But Jesus wants much more than that; he wants us in covenant with himself. I can have a personal relationship with the neighbor down the street; but that doesn't mean he wants me to move in and share his home. Likewise, Augustus

Caesar proclaimed himself to be Lord and Savior over all his subjects; but he didn't die on a cross so that they could become his brothers and sisters. Jesus Christ wants us in the New Covenant that he established through his own flesh and blood, the same covenant he renews through the Holy Eucharist. When his sacrifice for us is renewed at the altar, we gather at the family table for the sacred meal that makes us one. Jesus wants us to know not only the Father and the Holy Spirit but his Blessed Mother and all his sainted brothers and sisters as well. He also wants us to live according to the family structure he established for his Church on earth: the Pope and all the bishops and priests united to him. Come home to the Church established by Christ. Supper's waiting and the Savior's calling: "Behold, I stand at the door and knock; if anyone hears my voice and opens the door, I will come in to him and *eat* with him and he with me" (Rev 3:20).

Scott meeting the Holy Father, Pope John Paul II, for the first time. He is introduced by Kimberly's father, Dr. Jerry Kirk. January, 1992 at the Vatican.

To obtain audio and video cassette tapes
by Scott and Kimberly Hahn
covering a wide range of Scripture and Catholic doctrine,
as well as tapes by other inspired Catholic speakers,
contact:

St. Joseph's Communications, Inc.
P.O. Box 720
West Covina, CA 91793

800-526-2151
IN CALIFORNIA 818-331-3549